DEATH
THE FINAL SURRENDER

JESU XPI
PASSIO

by
Fr. Cedric Pisegna, C.P.

DEATH
THE FINAL SURRENDER

Praise be to You my Lord
For our sister bodily death
From whom no living man can flee.
Woe to those who die in mortal sin;
Blessed be those who are found
In your holy will
For the second death will not harm them.
Praise and bless my Lord and thank him
And serve him with great humility.
~St. Francis of Assisi~
The Canticle of the Creatures

FOREWORD

You may be wondering why I am writing a book about death. I hope to inspire you with the truths God has given me and to take away some of the mystery of death. When I was 20 years old, I had two experiences that turned my life around. These experiences happened within a few weeks of each other and were so similar that I will speak of both near death experiences as one singular experience.

Because of these touches of God, the way I view reality has changed. In these experiences, I was shown what happens when we die. Many have lost a parent, spouse or child to death and wonder where their loved one is. Others who were born Catholic do not know what our Church teaches about death. Some have been running from the reality of their impending death and need to face it.

There is a tremendous mystery enshrouding death. This mystery can bring about a lot of fear and confusion. It is said there are two things that we can be sure of in life: death and taxes. We are sure we are going to die yet we do not know the day or the hour. Not only do we not know when and where and how, we also do not know what happens when we die.

When I was on a two-week vacation I noticed something. The vacation lasted a good long time then suddenly it was over. Life is like that also. For most of us our life on earth lasts a good long time, then suddenly it ends. We must be prepared for this ending. Most prepare for their employment, financial future and retirement, but few prepare for their death although they know it is a certainty. Most fear and deny death but few face it.

I heard a story about a minister who waited in line to have his car filled with gas just before a long holiday weekend. The attendant worked quickly, but there were many cars ahead of him in line. Finally the attendant motioned the minister toward a now-vacant pump. "Reverend," said the young man, "Sorry about the delay. It seems as if everyone waits until the last minute to get ready for a long trip." The minister chuckled, "I know what you mean. It's the same in my business."

I am praying that the personal revelations I share in this book will ease your mind about the death experience. I share these experiences not to exalt myself, but to encourage you. I believe that death is the final healing. For Christians, death ought not to be dreaded but accepted and embraced as a means of our final growth and wholeness. The Christian journey of life is actually a pilgrimage of healings. When we follow Christ, we have a series of encounters with God; our death is the final one.

In addition, the purpose of this book is to help you to live well now and inspire you to prepare for your appointment with "sister" death. The Psalmist prayed, "Teach us to number our days that we may get a heart of wisdom." (Ps. 90:12) Instead of denying death, the Psalmist prayed to learn from the eventuality of his passing. The wisdom he was praying for was the tool he needed to live his life well. Wisdom is learning and growing from your own experiences as well as the experiences of others. Wisdom dictates that we live uprightly, love selflessly, and celebrate life now while we have it.

The Lord himself bless you with new insight, understanding, and a desire to give all to your call!

My prayers and love,

Fr. Cedric Pisegna, C.P.

1
DEATH: AN OVERVIEW

In the Bible, the book of Wisdom teaches us that "God did not make death and he does not delight in the death of the living." (Wis. 1:13) It is clear from the Scriptures that originally God created us to live forever. The Genesis story teaches us that because *we* chose to disobey, death entered into our experience. The first taste of death humanity encountered was separation from God. Guilt, shame and nakedness ensued. That blossomed into the cessation of life. "The wages of sin is death," Paul wrote the Church at Rome. (6:23) The fruit of disobedience is always death.

The dictionary defines death as "the permanent ending of all life in a person, animal or plant." This ending of life comes as a result of our misguided choices. But for Christians, the ending has now become a new beginning. Death has been transformed from an object of terror (the cessation of life) into a passageway of new life. During the Eucharistic prayer for the funeral Mass, something very beautiful is prayed. "Lord, for your faithful people, life is *changed*, not ended."

On the Cross, Jesus bore the full brunt of death's force. In a cosmic struggle, death sought to gain victory over God's Son. Jesus, the pioneer and the perfecter of our faith, was actually blazing a new trail for the rest of humanity. He conquered sin first and then the effect of sin, death. When he wrestled with death, he actually won the victory over it and transformed death into a rite of change, a new passageway. Rather than death being the time when life ceases, it has now become the time when life changes and a new life begins.

When Paul wrote his first letter to the Corinthians, he was discussing this very subject. Some of their number had died and those who lived wondered where they went and what happened to them. He spoke about death as an experience where we are changed, in the twinkling of an eye. Then in some of the most inspiring words in the whole of the New Testament, he wrote, "Death is swallowed up in victory. O death, where is your victory? O death, where is your sting?" (1 Cor. 15:54-55) These are tremendous words of truth and hope. Because of Jesus, death has now been transformed into the sphere of triumph and new life!

OTHER TRADITIONS

Of course not everyone believes what Christians do about death. People have various philosophies about what happens when we die. These ideas come from religion as well as culture. We are familiar with many of the notions. For example, atheists believe that when we die, that is the cessation of life as we know it. In the mind of an atheist, there is no afterlife or ultimate purpose. I saw a Christian bumper sticker that said, "Those who don't believe in an afterlife better hope they are right!"

On the other hand, most cultures believe in some form of an afterlife. I had the privilege of studying the Bible in Israel, Greece and Egypt in 1987. One place of particular interest to me is the Valley of the Kings and the tombs of some of the Egyptian pharaohs. They used to mummify the body and bury the body in a tomb. If the person was rich, the survivors would put his gold necklaces on the neck of the deceased person. His family and servants would adorn the dead body with all kinds of jewelry. Also, many of his possessions would be sealed in the tomb with the corpse. Egyptians believed that when the person came back to life, he or she would then have access to all these riches in the next life. They literally believed that "you *can* take it with you!"

Today there are many religions including Buddhism, Hinduism, Islam, New Age movements, Judaism, the Bahai faith, and Christianity. There is no "uniform" doctrine even within each of these religions. For example, Judaism at the time of Jesus was comprised of a number of sects. There were Sadducees who held that only the first five books of the Bible should form the foundation of Jewish life. They did not believe in the resurrection. The Pharisees were members of a lay reform movement who strictly upheld the law and the prophets. They did believe in an afterlife. The Essenes were a radical group who separated themselves from the mainstream and lived apart in their community near the Dead Sea. They were the authors of the Dead Sea Scrolls that have been so popularized today. They expected a Messiah who would be a righteous political warrior. Simon, one of the twelve apostles, was a zealot. Zealots were revolutionary Jews who sought to overthrow Roman domination by force. All these groups were Jewish, but their worship and beliefs differed. Even today there are many different styles and ways of being Jewish.

Similarly, any disciple of Jesus has a vast array of ways to express his or her devotion to Christ. There are scores of Christian denominations. The major division, of course, is between Catholicism and Protestantism. But even within Catholicism there have been splits. There are different rites and most Eastern Orthodox Catholics do not accept the authority of the Pope. Protestantism is broken up into many different denominations such as Baptist, Methodist and Lutheran. These various denominations all have their own style of liturgy and particular ways of believing.

When I describe some of the beliefs of a major religion, such as Buddhism for example, you must understand that within every religion there are a number of branches with varying beliefs. My intention is not to describe the subtleties of the branches but to summarize how various religions view death and the afterlife.

DON'T BE LED ASTRAY

I am familiar with some of the key tenets of the major religions in the world. It must be said that I am an outsider, writing about faiths of which I am not a part. I do not know all the subtleties of any other denomination the way I know my own. However, as I studied these religions and their views on the afterlife, I must tell you what rose up within me. It was similar to Paul's experience in Athens.

When Paul the Apostle came to Athens, Greece, he looked around the city and saw the people's devotion to various gods. As he looked around Athens he would have seen statues to Zeus, Poseidon, Hades, Aphrodite, and Hermes, among others. He even saw an altar inscribed to an "unknown god." When he saw all this, the Bible says that his spirit within him was "provoked." (Acts 17:16)

That is exactly how I feel when reading about various beliefs such as reincarnation, or soaring through higher planes, or New Ageism. Theological places of learning teach us tolerance and religious acceptance. While I agree with the importance of respecting another's tradition, it must be said that when I write about them here, I am in no way advocating any of these religions. I find myself very provoked within when I view some of the other denominations and their beliefs. I get upset because I feel many of their members are being deceived into believing lies. People are honestly searching for truth but are not finding it in all its fullness. Some innocently come to these religions and swallow error mixed with truth. They are passionate seekers who are not coming into contact with the whole truth. Paul wrote about some people having "zeal for God that is not enlightened." (Rom. 10:2)

For many people Christianity is simply lumped together with Buddhism and Islam as a "world religion." People see Jesus, Mohammed, Buddha and others as founders of religious movements and thus very similar. After all, they were all "good men."

It is clear to me that there are *vast* differences. Christianity stands alone as a religion that presents a means of redemption. Jesus is not a founder who is simply wise, so that if you follow his teaching you will be "enlightened." Rather it is through him, with him and in him that we come to God. He is the way. We must feed on his body and blood and remain in him. Rather than learning a way of wisdom alone, we are saved through a relationship with a living person, who we believe is God himself. For Christians, even prayer takes on a whole new meaning. For most religions, prayer is a means of gaining peace and coming to nirvana or self-knowledge. While this can happen in Christianity, prayer is primarily a *love-relationship* with the Holy Spirit. The whole thrust of Christianity is so different from other faiths. I am fond of quoting, "There is a big difference between Christianity and other religions. Religion is our search for God. Christianity is God's search for us."

Other religions and even other denominations within Christianity have elements of truth. But as I study them I discover much error mixed with truth. What happens is that people focus on the truth in their faith and miss the error. For example, as you will see, some religions believe in reincarnation. They rightly proclaim the truth that there is an afterlife. Naive people who want to believe in an afterlife but are undiscerning may swallow this easy doctrine whole.

From Christianity's perspective, reincarnation is simply false. Jesus never taught about it and if you study any of the canonized saints, you will see they never said a word about it. Surely God would have revealed this major truth to them if it were real! The truth as stated in the Bible is, "It is appointed for us to die *once* and after that comes judgment." (Heb. 9:27) People may concentrate on the truths in any specific religion (such as belief in an afterlife) and look for what sounds good and is easy to follow. To the undiscerning seeker, Christianity will always be just "one of the religions" out there. But to those reborn in the Holy Spirit, redeemed by the blood, and abiding in Christ, there are very few similarities. So, while I will fight for a person's freedom to choose, I am very cautious when people lump Christianity and other religions together. They are very different. If you are searching for a religion you can call your own, be very careful and very discerning. There are *vast* differences out there. That having been said, I would like to give a brief overview of some of the major religions and their beliefs about death and the afterlife.

VARIOUS VIEWS OF DEATH

Buddhists believe that when we die we are reincarnated. This belief is very appealing and many want to subscribe to it. I remember being so fascinated with this subject that I wrote a paper on it in high school. A recent Gallup poll showed that about 25% of the American people believe in some kind of reincarnation. I am aware of Catholics who know the basics of our faith, yet still believe in reincarnation. Perhaps one of the reasons it is so popular is because it lessens personal responsibility. If when we die we will simply come back again, why not live any way we want now? Things will turn out all right anyway. Granted, the object of reincarnation is to progress, but even if you don't you go forward in this life you will always have another chance.

One of my best friends, a Passionist missionary, is in India. I asked him, "What do the majority of people there believe?" He replied that the people there are mostly Hindus and they believe in reincarnation. He is working with our seminarians and priests trying to sow the Gospel in a foreign culture. Hindus see life as an illusion. They believe if you can just break through the illusions of this world, you can become enlightened. If a Hindu fails to find his or her true self in this world, he or she cycles through the wheel of death and rebirth. They keep being reincarnated until they find their true self. Although the body dies, the true self doesn't. Death is simply a pathway to reincarnation.

According to the Bahai faith, all world religions are of divine origin and differ only in non-essential doctrines. Adherents don't believe in reincarnation. They do believe in an afterlife and that we each have an everlasting soul. They see this world like our mother's womb and death as only a new birth. After death the soul embarks on a spiritual journey toward God.

Jews believe in an afterlife. Judaism teaches that when faithful people die they go to the abode of the righteous souls awaiting resurrection. If people did not study the law and did not seek God while alive, their souls will remain near their bodies in confusion and sadness. People's deeds, whether good or evil, will follow them. Jewish people believe that the Messiah is still to come. He will usher in a new age of peace and righteousness that will be a prelude to the resurrection. There will be a judgment, a resurrection and an afterlife. Heaven will be living with God forever.

In a similar way the followers of Islam believe in an afterlife. According to Islam there will be a resurrection, a judgment and a heaven and hell. People will be judged by their obedience to God's will on earth. These beliefs are similar to Christianity. A major difference is that Muslims believe that Jesus was only a prophet and not the Son of God.

2
WHAT DO CATHOLIC CHRISTIANS BELIEVE ABOUT DEATH?

It is clear that Jesus' life and mission pointed toward an afterlife. He taught about resurrection, heaven and hell. In fact, he made a claim that no one else in history has ever made: "I am the resurrection and the life, the one who believes in me, though he die, yet shall he live, and whoever lives and believes in me shall never die." (Jn. 11:25, 26) In the Nicene Creed we proclaim that "We look for the resurrection of the dead and the life of the world to come. Amen."

Christianity is a religion full of hope. Psalm 116:15 says, "*Precious* in the sight of the Lord is the death of one of his holy ones." God has his eye on the sparrow and he definitely has his eye on us. Our passing is precious to him!

Before I continue and write about death from a Christian perspective, I want to touch upon a *huge distinction*. Every other world religion focuses on a person coming to the afterlife through a cycle of rebirth or through obedience or even through following God's will. Christianity differs drastically in that the believer enjoys the afterlife *because of* Jesus. Not only has Jesus made a way for us, he *is* the way.

When Jesus died for us on the Cross he became our redemption from death. The power of death was broken. Through *him,* with *him* and in *him*, we can now live forever.

Our eternal life is not a result of our righteous deeds or obedience, although these traits distinguish a believer. Rather, it is because the Son of God, Jesus, loved us and gave himself for us. Our faith in him will give us life. Our acceptance of Jesus and his death on the Cross is our salvation. Paul the Apostle, who had a tremendous pedigree as a Jew, counted it all as rubbish in order to be found in Christ. (Phil. 3:7-9) No other religion comes close to believing that eternal life comes through belief in its founder. Christians aren't given life when they die as a natural part of a "rebirthing" process. They aren't awarded eternal life because they are good. Rather they receive the life that Jesus won for them because of their faith in Jesus' dying and rising.

THE MOMENT OF DEATH

As we end our liturgical year each November we focus on the "final things" which are death, judgment, heaven and hell. The readings at Mass concentrate on these areas. After we spend the final weeks of the liturgical year focusing on these truths, the season of Advent begins right where the end of the year left off: with the second coming of Jesus and the judgment. We begin and end the year with these truths because they are an extremely important part of the doctrine of our Catholic Christian faith.

The Catechism tells us that at the moment of death the soul is separated from the body. It will be reunited with the body on the day of the resurrection of the dead. (#1005) The Catechism further proclaims the truth that "Each man receives his eternal retribution in his immortal soul at *the very moment of his death*, in a particular judgment that refers his life to Christ: either entrance into the blessedness of heaven – through a purification or immediately – or immediate and everlasting damnation. (#1022) "But the souls of the righteous are in the hand of God and no torment will ever touch them." (Wis. 3:1) These teachings from the Catechism and the Scriptures tell us that at death there is an *immediate* coming before God. Our soul never dies. Each of us will either be at peace and in God's rest forever or will be separated in shame and disgrace. Our soul will be aware of its standing before God immediately at death. There is no time of non-being and then resurrection. Death is but a passageway to eternity. St. Therese of Lisieux said, "I am not dying; I am entering life."

TRANSITUS

The feast day of St. Francis of Assisi is October 4th. Many people bring their animals in for a special blessing on that day. On the eve of his feast day, Franciscans and others who mark Francis' passing celebrate "transitus" or Francis' transition from life on earth to eternal life. That's exactly what death is for a Christian. It is a transition from this life to the blessed life to come.

On Ash Wednesday priests make the Sign of the Cross with ashes on our forehead and say, "Remember, man, that you are dust and to dust you shall return." Those stark, sobering words are meant to help us remember our end and choose God's way to live our life. Death is that moment that ends a person's ability to choose or reject God. Your prior faith, works, deeds, choices and personhood follow you at the moment of your death. How you accepted and believed in God's grace offered to you will determine your eternal destiny. If you believed in Jesus' sacrificial death for you and showed that faith by loving him and obeying his teachings, you will live. Those who did not accept Jesus and rejected the belief that he died for their sins will face the terror of a just judgment. The Bible warns, "It is a fearful thing to fall into the hands of the living God." (Heb. 10:31) The same Bible, however, invites us to remember that God is very merciful and "mercy triumphs over judgment." (Jas. 2:13)

There is a deep curiosity and fascination with the death experience. As I write this book, there is a popular show on T.V. called "Crossing Over." The host of this program claims to be able to make contact with loved ones who have died. The ratings are high because members of the audience and viewers at home want to know what has happened to those who have died. Some turn to psychics, mediums and the occult to try to contact a deceased loved one. This is strictly forbidden in the Bible. In fact, through the witch of Endor, King Saul once consulted the dead prophet Samuel. Partly because of this, he was told that God had taken his kingdom from him and that he would die the next day. (1 Sam. 28:15-19) The occult may seem innocent and harmless, but those who participate in it are toying with evil.

TEARS IN HEAVEN?

For Christians, the journey of our life here on earth is a pilgrimage toward heaven. Heaven is our true home. "Our commonwealth is in heaven." (Phil. 3:20) Those who die in the grace of Christ will know the joy of paradise.

Heaven is a place where we will be with Christ forever and see God face-to-face. We call this the beatific vision. God will no longer be hidden, but we will know God in an intensely personal way. The Bible promises that then we will know as we are known. (1 Cor. 13:12) I always picture heaven as a place of rapture, joy and being able to do whatever you want. People now like to eat, golf, travel, garden, shop, visit, and talk. Imagine the new delights God will give to his people. Try to imagine new sports and hobbies and interests that we have never even thought of! Try to dream of new tastes, scents and sights. Picture fabulous golf courses with crystal clear waterfalls, colorful leaves and no crowds. In heaven, there will be no more depression, discouragement or disappointment. Sickness and death will flee. Peace will flow like a river. Finally we will have peace and quiet. No more mowers, blowers, trash trucks or barking dogs. Life will be as it was originally meant to be. Eden will be restored.

One of my favorite activities on earth is eating. I love to eat. Apparently Jesus did too. One scripture commentator on the Gospel of Luke humorously wrote that Jesus must have been fat because most of the time he is at a meal or talking about food! The prophet Isaiah was a painter. In his prophecy about heaven he painted a portrait of a great banquet. "On this mountain the Lord of hosts will make for all peoples a feast of rich food and choice wines, juicy, rich food and pure, choice wines." (Is. 25:6) Jesus himself described heaven as a wedding feast given by a great king for his son. "Come to the feast!" Jesus invites. (Mt. 22:4) Imagine your favorite foods and drink: Yankee pot roast, corn on the cob, mashed potatoes, strawberry shortcake with ice cream and whipped cream! We will drink the best $10,000-a-bottle delicious wine. Another benefit will be that we won't have to worry about cholesterol and we will never grow fat. Non-guilt feasting!

The Bible teaches that we will be caught up in the ecstasy of worshipping God face-to-face. Finally we will see God as he is and praise him endlessly for his goodness to us. (Rev. 4:1 to 5:14) The finest worship experiences we have ever attended will pale in comparison to the worship to come.

One of the greatest joys will be the reunion we will have with our dead loved ones. When I lost my dad to death, one of the thoughts that comforted me was, "I'll see you later." That one thought helped me more than anything else to grieve well. The Bible assures us there will be no more pain or death and "God will wipe away every tear from our eyes!" (Rev. 21:4) If you want an imaginative description of the delights of heaven, read chapters 21 and 22 in the Book of Revelation. The Bible concludes with an invitation to all to enjoy the gift of heaven. "The Spirit and the Bride say, 'Come.'" (Rev. 22:17) What an invitation! Our hope in heaven should inspire and color every day of our life here on earth. Hope isn't just for the hereafter, but for the here and now. Because of hope we can cope.

One of the truths the Lord impressed on my heart about heaven is that we must realize that it won't be for just a little while. Heaven will last forever and ever and ever! It is vitally necessary that you come to Christ and know that you will live eternally.

The opening prayer for the Solemnity of the Assumption of Mary is telling. On that great feast day we pray, "May we see heaven as our final goal." Do you have heaven as a goal? Most of us have some sort of nebulous idea of what heaven is and never really strive for it. Most hope they are going there but don't know for sure. A goal is something you have set before you every day. Paul told the Colossians to "set your minds on the things that are above." (3:2) Because heaven is our goal we are determined to receive it. Our goal will influence our behaviors and activities. Heaven will influence the way we think and dream. As believers, heaven must be our final goal. Live a determined life striving and seeking, pressing on toward your final goal.

In Christ you can know you are going to heaven. This is not presumption, but blessed assurance. You don't have to wish or hope or think "maybe." One of the joys Jesus came to bring is that we would know our names are written in heaven. The Spirit bears witness to this truth. Paul tells us that "what no eye has seen nor ear heard . . . God has revealed to us in the Spirit!" (1 Cor. 2:9) A spirit-filled person ought to have a sense of his or her eternal destiny and not be confused. In my book *Glorious Holy Spirit,* I describe how one of the roles of God's Spirit is to bear witness to your innermost self that you are saved and on the way to heaven. If you have committed your life to Christ and know his Holy Spirit, you are a child of God now. Eternal life has already begun. Your death will be but a passageway to your inheritance!

I'M TOO YOUNG TO DIE!

Many of those who die in Christ are saved, yet are still in need of further purification. We all have the experience of loving God, yet still having sin, selfishness and compromise in our hearts. None of us loves others as we should. We all need to be purged of narcissism and selfishness. Who among us is totally surrendered to Christ? Some need more time because their experiences are not complete. Life on earth now is a time of being made holy and being purified from our sins. The reason we are being cleansed now is so that we will be able to stand before God when we die and our capacity to receive him will be all the greater. The Catholic Church teaches there is a place called purgatory wherein the elect, the saved, will have more time to be transformed. This purification process is not a time when a soul "works" to earn heaven. Those deemed worthy of purgatory are already forever saved. (I will discuss having been justified and yet still being justified at a later time.) Rather, it is a place of grace to give those who need to grow and be cleansed further time to be changed. Scripture refers to the cleansing of the afterlife in several places. (2 Macc. 12:46, 1 Cor. 3:15, 1 Pet. 1:7, and Mt. 12:31)

How long will this take? What kind of a place is purgatory? No one knows for sure. Try not to think of it as a terrible place of flames. Remember, it is a place of grace. Just as God's grace works in us now to consecrate us to God, so grace will continue to be active in those who die in Christ. The "poor" souls in purgatory are really quite rich. They are saved and being purified. We can pray for them.

Some have a problem with purgatory. They ask, "If you are saved then what more do you need?" It is clear to me that not everyone saved is perfect. We still need to be transformed. While our bodies may be changed "in the twinkling of an eye" (1 Cor. 15:52) the transformation of our hearts takes time.

The doctrine of purgatory makes total sense to me when I look at my own experience. I know I am being pruned and dealt with now by God. I am saved and I hope that the sufferings and trials and circumstances I am enduring now will do their perfect work in me. (Rom 5:1-5, Jas. 1:2-4) When I die, I want to be perfect and complete and lacking in nothing. Isn't this the goal of your life? In purgatory we will be sanctified (made holy) so that we can stand before God and receive God more fully. Mercifully, we will be given more time to complete our purification process. I leave you with this Bible quote that attests to the truth of purification. "For he is like a refiner's fire and like fuller's soap; he will sit as a refiner and purifier of silver, and he will purify the sons of Levi and refine them like gold and silver, till they present right offerings to the Lord." (Mal. 3:2-3)

HELL

In May of 2002 I had the privilege of leading 25 people on pilgrimage to the shrines of Italy. One of the highlights of our trip to Rome was a tour of the Vatican museum. When we entered the Sistine Chapel we marveled at the recently restored frescos of Michelangelo. On the back wall we could see the stunning *Last Judgment*. As I examined the murals, Christ stood out at the center as judge. On his right were the saved, but on his left were those damned to punishment in hell. It was a terrible scene of demons, snakes and looks of horrific anguish on people's faces. Hell, as portrayed by Michelangelo, is a place of utter chaos and terror.

All of us have choices in life and there are eternal *consequences* to our choices. We have all been given the grace of life and will have to account for this indescribable gift. With grace comes responsibility. Many today are living for themselves. They convince themselves they care for others but do little to help anyone. They always live intending to get involved, but many never really do. Perhaps the saying *is* true, "The road to hell is paved with good intentions."

Most believe God exists, but few give their lives to him. People sin constantly and some of those sins are grave. Many keep on sinning because time passes and there seems to be no punishment. They interpret this lack of immediate consequences as a sign they are as getting by with what they do. From God's point of view, he is mercifully giving us time so that we will return to him. Make no mistake about it: there will be a day of reckoning. The sinful side of us loves to gamble, but the spiritual side is an investor. Don't gamble with your eternal destiny! If you continue to live in a state of selfishness, sin, and lack of trust in God, you will be separated from God here on earth. God is constantly holding out his love and grace for a person to accept. If a person continues to reject and ignore the free gift of God, there will come a time when that grace will be withdrawn. "*Today* is the day of salvation. *Now* is the acceptable time." (2 Cor. 6) "Come to me," Jesus beckons to all.

THE ULTIMATE REJECTION

God doesn't so much send people to hell as people, through multiple decisions throughout their life, separate themselves from God now and thus into eternity. "To die in mortal sin without repenting and accepting God's merciful love means remaining separated from him forever by our own free choice. This state of definitive self-exclusion from communion with God and the blessed is called 'hell.'" (*Catechism* #1033)

One of the most unforgettable hurts I have ever endured is that of rejection. I remember a relationship I had with a woman in college. We dated for almost a year. We grew very close and were emotionally attached. Toward the end of the relationship, I grew dissatisfied and ended up breaking off the relationship. I searched my heart deep within and sensed she was not the one I wanted to marry.

However, I still loved her and she loved me. The breakup itself was very painful, but I knew it was for the best. Some time later, in my loneliness, I tried to get back together with her. She was already dating someone else and I felt rejected and not accepted by the woman I had loved and who had loved me. I knew it was now too late to get her back and I had to suffer the pain of loss and separation. The pain of knowing that she was with someone else was unbearable. The irony of this pain was that through my own choices, I brought it upon myself! It was a bitter pain and I will never forget how hard that was. She did not belong to me anymore and I did not belong to her. Imagine the pain of being rejected and separated forever from the one who gave you life itself and truly loves you. Whether we know it or not we make a break from God when we sin, doubt him, and neglect the nearness of his presence. Exclusion from God because of our own choices will be more than anyone can bear. We call this agony hell.

The Church has always taught that hell is real and eternal. The chief punishment of hell is exclusion from God and the shame that results. Perhaps the burning of hell won't be the flames of fire. Have you ever felt the burning in your face when you blush from shame or embarrassment? Imagine the burning you will feel within your soul when you realize that because of your choices you managed to exclude love itself from your life and thus destroyed your eternal destiny. The fire of hell will be the burning of shame, regret, anguish and embarrassment as you realize that your life was a travesty.

Even though you will long to be a part of the people of God and enjoy the delights of heaven, it will be too late. (Lk. 16:26) The incomparable gift of life was wasted. You have little virtue to show for your life. You did not seek or love God. You realize that this precious gift, now lost, was in vain. Then you will see God in all his majesty and the rewards of all those who love him and you know you will be excluded from this forever. Hell is the absence of God and of love. Beware of those who preach there is no hell because it doesn't make sense to them. Beware also of those who use hell as a swear word (possibly revealing where they are headed). Scripture, tradition and the saints have all taught the reality of hell. Jesus himself sadly predicted, "There you will weep and gnash your teeth, when you see Abraham and Isaac and Jacob and all the prophets in the kingdom of God and you yourselves thrust out." (Lk. 13:28)

THE DAY OF THE LORD (JL. 2:31)

Many times in Scripture we are given a warning about "the day of the Lord." This day of vengeance and wrath has been predicted many times by various authors of the Bible. The prophet Joel predicted it will be a great and terrible day. Before this day, the sun will be turned to darkness and the moon to blood. (Jl. 2:31) The prophet Amos predicted it will be a day of darkness not light. (Am. 5:18) The book of Revelation with its symbolic imagery foretells the wrath of God. (Rev. 6:16-17) Jesus himself predicted wars, famines, earthquakes and then the end. He warned us to be ready for it although no one knows the day or the hour. (Mk. 24:7, 36) Peter wrote, "The day of the Lord will come like a thief, and then the heavens will pass away with a loud noise, and the elements will be dissolved with fire, and the earth and the works that are upon it will be burned up." (2 Pet. 3:10)

There is a popular belief that the consummation of the world will occur through people. The world is full of tension, wars and pollution. We see terrorism, murder, poverty and hunger. People are narcissistic and self-indulgent. The Scriptures make it clear that although people will contribute to hastening the end of the world, *God himself* will usher in the end. God began the world and God will end it. God is the Alpha and the Omega (the beginning and the end). (Rev. 22:13) Many today live as if the world will never end. Denying what is to come or being ignorant of it will not change the facts. Every Advent we hear about the end of the world and hear the stern and profound warning of Jesus, "Watch, be ready and be prepared!" (Mk. 13:33) In the words of Peter, "Since all these things are thus to be dissolved, what sort of persons ought you to be in lives of holiness and godliness, waiting for and hastening the coming of the day of God." (2 Pet. 3:11) Thus the end calls us to new beginnings in our behaviors.

It has been predicted over and over again in the Scriptures and our liturgies. A day *is* coming: the day of the Lord. In the seminary I learned that every prediction Jesus ever made has already come true, except one: his second coming. We believe that his prophecy will one day be fulfilled. In the words of the Creed that we recite every Sunday at Mass, "He (Jesus) will come again in glory to judge the living and the dead and his kingdom will have no end." This will be a world-wide event and every person on the face of the earth will see his astounding appearance. "Behold, he is coming with the clouds, and every eye will see him, every one who pierced him; and all tribes of the earth will wail on account of him. Even so. Amen." (Rev. 1:7) The Bible ends with the great cry of the early Church, *Maranatha*, "Come, Lord Jesus!" (Rev. 22:20)

THE LAST JUDGMENT

Scripture also teaches that after the consummation of the world at the end of time, there will be a resurrection and a last judgment. That last judgment will occur at the second coming of Jesus. Although there has already been an individual judgment at the moment of death, this verdict will be ratified at the throne of God. Every person who ever lived will be reunited with his or her body at the resurrection and stand before the great white throne of God. We will be judged by our deeds as well as whether or not we are in the "book of life." (Rev. 20:11-15)

Once when Jesus' disciples returned from a healing campaign, they were rejoicing because of all they had done. Jesus told them to rejoice rather "that your names are written in heaven." (Lk.10:20) This "Lamb's book of the living" (Rev. 13:8) includes all those who have given their lives to Jesus, trusting in him for salvation. Included are those justified by the blood sacrifice of Jesus on the Cross. Salvation, of course, is a free gift to be accepted by faith. Revelation speaks of other "books" that will be opened on that day, books that contain a record of the deeds that are the fruit and confirmation of our faith. The way we live is the showing forth of our justification in Christ. If we truly believe in Christ, love, honesty, generosity and integrity will characterize our deeds. These deeds don't save us, but will be the warrant of the rewards we will receive in heaven. Jesus made it clear in many places that rewards will follow our deeds. (Mt. 5:12, 16:27)

Imagine the scene: you will be standing shoulder to shoulder with every person who has ever lived. Billions upon billions will stand before God. There will be a huge gathering of saints and sinners. You will see many ushered into the glory of heaven. You will see still others dying the second death forever. At that moment, you will long to have lived a life of excellence and integrity. Those who lived in faith and obedience will be guarded and given a beautiful crown. (Pr. 4:6,9) Your commitment to Christ will flower in blessing and protection. God will be looking for fruit from your life. The fruit I refer to is a right relationship with God, the fruit of the Holy Spirit, and the fruit of impacting people for Christ. "Blessed are the dead who die in the Lord . . . for their deeds follow them!" (Rev. 14:13)

The Scriptures speak of a "second" death (Rev. 20:14) that we must avoid at all costs. This second death is the result of God's judgment and is irreversible. All who are not in Christ and in God's grace will be separated from God forever. The primary choice that we make for or against Christ, as well as the choices made each day that proceed from this fundamental decision, will determine our destiny.

JUDGMENT IS NOW

The Gospel of John gives us a nuanced theology of the judgment. For John the judgment is *now* as well as still to come. This "realized eschatology" can be seen in John 3:19-21. In these verses John speaks about choices and deeds as the determining factor of our judgment. Make no mistake about it, the choices we make and the way we live our life *now* have everything to do with eternity. Sow good seed by the way you live now and don't sabotage your life with foolish choices that will come back to haunt you.

All who are in Christ and are written in the Lamb's book of life will live forever with God in the delights of heaven. On that day there will be a great divide. (Mt. 25:31-46) Believers who expressed their faith through good deeds and caring for people will experience the blessedness of heaven. Everyone who has ever lived and who will ever live will stand before the judgment seat of God. "In the presence of Christ, who is the Truth itself, the truth of each one's relationship with God will be laid bare." (*Catechism* #1038)

Being aware of the truths of our faith is not enough. Eternity, heaven, hell, and the last judgment are not just sobering truths to assent to. These truths call us to live with faith, integrity and love. These truths demand accountability and responsibility. We have time now. Just how much time we have no one knows. The time God gives us on earth is a gift to us for which we are responsible. We must *choose* life in order to live. Death and the judgment of God are certain. How we will respond to it varies from person to person. Jesus taught, "As it was in the days of Noah, so will it be in the days of the Son of Man. They ate, they drank, they married, they were given in marriage, until the day when Noah entered the ark, and the flood came and destroyed them all." (Lk. 17:26-27)

GIVE YOUR LIFE TO JESUS

Are you ready for judgment day? Is your name written in the Lamb's book of life? If you have given your life to Jesus and believe he died for you on the Cross, you have already come to new life. Others are not ready. Many people just go about their business as usual and death will catch them off guard. But for those who are wise and discerning, solid choices about God are being made now. I pray that the truths written about here will not just bring understanding. Rather, I pray they will help motivate you to be responsible for your eternal destiny by giving your life to Jesus and making solid godly choices in your everyday life.

One of the main purposes of this book is to help you to make sure you know where you are going. Salvation comes through giving your life to Jesus. You must believe that he went to the Cross and died for your sins out of love for you. It is your faith in Jesus and what he did for you that will save you. Then you must live for Jesus. The process of salvation and justification will then be "worked out" in your soul and heart. You must be transformed into his image.

You can certainly come to Christ in your own prayer time. Surrendering to Jesus at communion or through the sacrament of confession is wonderful too. The important thing is that you make a definitive decision for Jesus and choose him as your savior. One other way this can be done is by praying this simple prayer. It's not saving in and of itself; rather, it is your committing yourself to Jesus in faith that is saving. Please pray from your heart.

Jesus, I believe you love me
and died on the Cross for me.
I come to you just as I am.
I surrender my life to you.
I want to know you and follow you.
Because of your love for me,
I believe I am written in your book of the living!
I believe I am saved and going to heaven.
I love you Lord Jesus.
Amen!

Express your surrender to Jesus by worshipping him at church. Grow in Jesus by praying and reading the Bible and other spiritual books. Get involved in the community and reach out to others. May you truly know the joy of the

Lord and the assurance of everlasting salvation in your heart of hearts. Death for you will be a coming home. God bless you and touch you right now!

In the future realize that when you come to communion you are receiving the body and blood of Jesus who gave himself to you. It's not just a ritualistic action that we routinely do. His body and blood are salvific. Just before we distribute communion, priests pray, "May the body and blood of Christ bring us to everlasting life. Amen."

If you are wearing a cross or have a crucifix on your wall, look at it for what it really is. The cross displays God's love for you and is a reminder of your salvation. We Passionists wear a cross over our heart. It is called our sign. Jesus did signs in the Gospels. These actions were miraculous deeds that touched people and brought them to faith. The ultimate sign is the cross. The cross is "the miracle of miracles," as St. Paul of the Cross termed it. This "sign of the Son of Man" (Mt. 24:30) that Jesus spoke of should be in our heart, not just over it. Therefore Passionists have a saying, "May the Passion of Jesus Christ be always *in* our hearts." I pray that you will know the saving power of the Cross as you give your life to Christ. It is the sign that you are loved and saved.

3
THE DEATH EXPERIENCE

Recently I represented our religious community and the Catholic Church as a whole at a Hispanic job fair. The event was held at the George R. Brown Convention Center in downtown Houston. There were probably 9,000 Hispanic young people who were bussed in from the surrounding areas of Houston. Different corporations such as Krogers and I.B.M and many colleges had set up booths to try to attract the young people. As part of my quest for vocations, I went to this fair hoping to attract some young people to consider a vocation to the priesthood. I was the lone Catholic priest there and had a booth simply called "Catholic Church." I brought with me many brochures to hand out about the priesthood.

At noontime I went to eat lunch. My priestly collar attracted the eye of a 20-year-old young man. He came over to me and introduced himself. As we began to talk, he said, "Since the events of September 11th I've really been doing a lot of soul-searching about life and death. I'm not really sure what happens when we die. I don't go to church but I know I need more of God in my life." I talked to him about God. I mentioned that his hunger was drawing him to know God in a deeper way.

After the terrorist attacks of September 11th, many are in the same boat as this young man. People are examining life more closely. Suddenly mortality is no longer an abstract idea. All of a sudden death is too close. It was horrific to watch as almost 3,000 people died on that terrible day. For a while church attendance was up. Bible sales increased. Airplane and travel reservations were way down. People were thinking about death and wondering how their own lives will end. Scores were looking for security and answers.

It is *right* that we should search and look for answers and be curious about death. Although no one knows the day or the hour, our Church offers us many answers about death and the afterlife. It is crucial that we explore and know what the Church teaches. If we make good choices and live well now, we will be prepared for the inevitability of death.

We live in a death-denying culture. Many elderly are sent away to homes and removed from the mainstream of community. The emphasis is on exercise, drugs and staying eternally young. Most don't want to spend time thinking about their mortality. Considering the end can lead to despair, confusion and doubt. While the reality of death is denied on one hand, on the other hand it is also blown out of proportion in the media. Movies and T.V. shows often make fun of death or so exploit violence and murder that we become numb to death's reality. News shows constantly display all that is negative in society. Whether the news we tune in to is national or local, murders, killings, kidnappings and death seem to always permeate the headlines.

Our Church doesn't deny or overstate death; rather, it looks death square in the face. We proclaim the inevitability of death and teach that we should learn from it and prepare for it. Scholars tell us that the Passion narratives were the earliest kernels of the Gospels written. The rest of the Gospel accounts grew up around the record of Jesus' death. One of the first things the early Church had to deal with was the scandal of its leader being put to death. The Church didn't deny the Passion of Jesus, but faced this truth and used it as the center of its life-transforming message. Jesus' death led to forgiveness and new life for all. The font and summit of a Catholic's life is the Mass which proclaims the death of the Lord until he comes again. Our Church calls us to reflect upon our own impending death and to live faithfully. Far from leaving us orphans and in confusion, the Catholic Church has well-defined teachings regarding death and the afterlife.

I have reflected a lot on the death experience. We don't know how or where or when we are going to die, but we do know *that* death is in our future. I have been taken many times to play golf at the Lake Charles Country Club in Louisiana. The first hole is a par five with an intriguing hazard. Just to the left of the green is a graveyard. If you pull your approach shot at all your ball will end up in the cemetery. While I was playing golf, the thought came to me that even when I am out enjoying the beauty of golf, the reality of death is ever present.

Our Church teaches us to get back to basics and reflect on our end. I have explored many teachings from a wide variety of traditions and religious circles. Those who search will find a wealth of information about death and the afterlife. Some of it is solid and orthodox while other teachings are strange and confusing. Discernment is necessary.

Two of the most fascinating books about the afterlife have been written by Raymond A. Moody, Jr., M.D. I have read *Life After Life* and *The Light Beyond.* In addition I have read the New York Times #1 bestseller by Betty J. Eadie called *Embraced by the Light.* Another astonishing religious book you may want to explore is *Heaven: Close Encounters of the God Kind* by Rev. Jesse Duplantis. These books all explore the experience of death in a unique way.

Dr. Moody has encountered a number of people who have had what he terms "near-death experiences." He compiled many cases of those who had experienced the death phenomenon. These people fell into distinct categories. First, there were those who were thought to be dead and who were resuscitated. Secondly, people who had been through car accidents, heart attacks or operations and who came close to physical death were interviewed. Thirdly, he includes those who actually died and told the people at their side about their experience of dying.

COMMON ELEMENTS OF
NEAR-DEATH EXPERIENCES

There seemed to be common elements in the experiences of the people he studied. First of all, after the accident or operating table experience, the person had the sensation of leaving the body. Some were able to observe themselves on the operating table after they left their body, and even to hear the doctor pronounce them dead! If this sounds fantastically strange to you, listen to these words from the Scriptures themselves: "I know a man [Paul himself] who fourteen years ago was caught up to the third heaven – whether in the body or out of the body I do not know, God knows. And I know that this man was caught up into Paradise – whether in the body or out of the body I do not know, God knows – and he heard things that cannot be told, which man may not utter." (2 Cor. 12:2-4) I believe that Paul was describing an out-of-body experience here.

The second common element of a near-death experience is the tunnel. After leaving the body the person has the sensation of being pulled or sucked through some type of a tunnel, funnel, cylinder or vacuum. This passageway is the transition place between life on earth and the afterlife.

Next there is an encounter with the divine being. Most describe God as a being of light. There is a sense of his personality and goodness and love. This light is dazzling and glorious. People from varying religious backgrounds describe the being as God, Christ, an angel, or simply a being. The being usually does not communicate with the person in an audible voice, but through the transference of thoughts. Often people are asked questions such as, "Are you ready to die? Have you lived a worthy life? What have you done with your life? How have you loved?" The questions are asked not so much in condemnation as in love.

Fourth comes the judgment or life review. Perhaps you've heard of a person who had an accident or incident in which their life "passed before them." In a word, that is what happens before the being of light. Suddenly and quickly and without compromise, the individual's life is replayed before him or her. Some say their whole life was reviewed, while others claim that it was just the highlights. But all agree that it is quick and thorough and unarguable. The conclusion drawn by some who have experienced this is that the being of light is trying to show them that the meaning of life is to love others and acquire knowledge. This life review is a means of helping to motivate the person to do just that.

Next comes the sensation of returning to the body. Many report they feel the beam of light has allowed them to return to live on earth again. Some didn't want to leave the light, but knew they had to. Once again there is the sensation of being pulled through some type of tunnel and returning to the body. When they do, suddenly they are back on the operating table, in the car accident or wherever they were as if no time had passed.

The final common element reported is a changed life. Transformation results because the person who had the near-death experience knows what has happened to them was real. Life takes on new meaning and becomes greatly appreciated and precious. An important fruit of the near-death experience is the understanding that loving other people is required of each of us. Just as the being of light loved them with generosity and warmth, so now those touched by that love want to love others in return. The need to learn was also expressed. Growing and learning are processes that continue even into the afterlife. Because of their new lease on life, these people tend to take advantage of every opportunity to expand their knowledge.

NO MORE FEAR

As you might imagine, after an experience like this the fear of death is lessened or removed. The book of Hebrews tells us that Jesus came to "deliver all those who through fear of death were subject to lifelong bondage." (Heb. 2:15) Some time ago a friend of mine told me about his mother. She had been Catholic all her life and as he put it, "She was the rock of my faith." One evening they had a discussion wherein she confessed her doubts and fears having to do with death. It caused a lot of confusion in my friend, because he had always looked to his mother for strength. Even some very holy people are afraid of dying.

Much of the fear stems from the unknown. There is confusion. "What will happen?" people wonder. "Will it hurt? Will I simply cease to be? Will I panic and have feelings of suffocation?" I received a letter from a woman who attended a mission I preached in Placerville, California. She wrote, "Although I believe and do trust, I am afraid of death and the thought of eternity. I am 37 years old and this has been a concern of mine for at least the last 25 years. Because I am so uneasy with the thought of death, I need your prayers. I need the peace and joy that can only come from above." Another woman told me that she suffered panic attacks whenever she would think about dying. She isn't sure what happens at the moment of death. That fear causes terror in her mind.

In the near-death experience, much of the mystery of death is revealed to the person and he or she no longer fears the unknown. Most who have had near death-experiences talk about death as a transition or an entry to another state of consciousness. Since they have already experienced going through death, there is new peace in their minds about it. You may wonder, "Why haven't I had a near-death experience?" Some need it because of their sinful and selfish state; others encounter death because of an unforeseen accident and still others because of the gift of God to them. Anyone who has such an experience has to interpret it for him or herself. Whether or not you have had this experience yourself (and I know some of you have) I am praying that you will experience it vicariously through this book. As the Holy Spirit confirms the truth of what I am writing here, I pray that you will be untroubled as you think about your own death as well as the death of your loved ones. I also hope you will be motivated to love others now and to grow by learning more on your own personal journey.

4
REBORN

Many have written about their own faith experience. All report that words do not suffice. Language is not sufficient to try to describe the transcendent. For example, after St. Thomas Aquinas had written volumes and volumes of learned works, this famous Doctor of the Church had an encounter with God. When he met God in a powerful way the experience left him breathless. He looked back at his philosophizing and reasoning. He had spent countless hours writing and pouring his heart into his works. "All is straw," he wrote. His religious experience made him realize the immensity and the profundity of God as well as his own inadequacy to reflect on God. "My thoughts are not your thoughts and neither are your ways my ways, says the Lord." (Is. 55:8) An encounter with God is beyond words, but nevertheless, words are a medium of communication by which one can try to convey meaning and experience. We must not give up trying to probe the meaning and the depths of God. Words are inadequate, but they're all we have. With that in mind, I attempt to share with you what happened to me.

My evening began simply enough. It was July in 1977 and I was a 20-year-old college student. I had just completed my sophomore year. I was at my parents' house in Massachusetts, home on summer break, and was simply lying on the living room floor watching a Boston Red Sox baseball game on T.V. This had been a summer of searching for me. Those of you who know my story know that about a year earlier I began waking up in the morning and looking around wondering, "What is all this?"

As I would sit on the side of my bed I had thoughts like, "I'm not happy. I feel like I'm missing something. I know there is more to life than what I have. I'm not satisfied." I didn't try to think those thoughts, they just came. A wonderful truth about God is that he will make you hungry even though you don't know what you are hungry for.

Since this kept happening day after day, I began to do something about the voice of my conscience that kept beckoning to me. One of the first things I did was to read the Bible. Although I had been born and brought up Catholic, I had fallen away from participating in the Church. I had Christianity as my foundation, but it was not an ongoing reality in my life. Part of the teaching I had received was that truth is found in the Scriptures. I've heard it said that the letters in the word Bible stand for: Basic Information Before Leaving Earth. I came to the Bible wide-eyed and open. I was motivated to read what Jesus taught about life. What answers did he have? I wanted to have what I sensed I was missing, even though I didn't know what it was. My interior hunger energized me and kept me looking.

My search brought me back to the basics of Christianity. I began to pray. I read the Scriptures. As I prayed and read, my faith grew. I believed that God was there and I began to develop a relationship with him. The same God that I had heard others talk about was now becoming *my* God.

Faith is a force within. Faith emanates from the deep recesses of the heart. It is primarily a gift from God, but it must be nourished and fed. In Mark's Gospel, Jesus tells two parables about faith. The first is a parable about sowing seeds. "The kingdom of God is as if a man should scatter seed upon the ground, and should sleep and rise night and day, and the seed should sprout and grow, he knows not how. The earth produces of itself, first the blade, then the ear, then the full grain in the ear." (Mk. 4:26-28) The seed of faith will grow of itself when prayer, God's word, obedience and worship nourish it. As I woke up each morning, prayed, read, lived and went back to bed day in and day out, faith was growing of itself.

ONLY BELIEVE

Faith is a gift that starts as a very small thing. It is simply the urge within you to believe in God and trust that he is there and wants to be gracious to you. That thought or force or thrust within can quickly become very large. It can consume you and be the driving force of your life. The other parable Jesus told relating to faith was, "The kingdom of God is like a grain of mustard seed, which when sown upon the ground, is the smallest of all the seeds on earth; yet when it is sown it grows up and becomes the greatest of all shrubs, and puts forth large branches, so that the birds of the air can make nests in its shade." (Mk. 4:31-32) My faith began as an exploratory search. It started as energy to seek God. Before I knew it, faith became my whole life. The entire direction of my life, my call and my life's energies are all caused and directed by my faith in God. I have been reborn and saved because of faith. My branches are growing and others are nesting in the shade of my ministry and their faith is being nourished there. Faith is vitally important!

Remember, faith is a *gift* and begins as energy within you to seek God. No matter how far along you are in your walk with God, faith will still lead you to search for God. You must not give up the search because of some initial "finds." You can't just rest on yesterday's laurels. Faith will drive you your whole life long to mine the treasures of God.

Faith will also lead you as you continue your journey. We walk by faith from beginning to end.

Faith is one of the virtues that lasts forever. It is a confidence, an assurance, and a conviction regarding things not seen. Without faith, it is impossible to please God, for whoever would draw near to God must believe that he exists and that God rewards those who seek him. (Heb. 11:6) I invite you to build up your faith by exploring chapter 11 of the letter to the Hebrews. The author extols many characters of the Bible and demonstrates how they lived lives of victory and blessing because of faith.

Because of the faith that God was inspiring within me, I had begun a search for God. Paul told the Athenians that God created them so "they should seek God, in the hope they might feel after him and find him." (Acts 17:27) For about nine months I had been feeling and groping and searching for God. My faith was growing. I didn't give up and remained persistent in my pursuit of God.

Years ago people put bumper stickers on their cars that read, "I found it!" They were referring to finding eternal life through Jesus. In my view, it ought to have read, "I've been found." The first version puts the emphasis on us, the second rightly places the emphasis on grace. Even though we do the seeking, it is God who does the finding. Three famous lost and found stories are proclaimed in Luke 15. All have to do with God's search for us, the outpouring of grace, and joy at the finding. In the song "Amazing Grace" we sing, "I once was lost but now I'm found." That night in July, I was about to be found.

As I lay there on the floor watching the ballgame that evening, suddenly I began to get a stomach-ache and decided to go to bed early. I had no idea of the life-changing experience that was about to occur. I don't even remember if I prayed that night as I went to bed.

THE TUNNEL

I was drifting off to sleep when I suddenly felt myself being pulled down a passageway. I was very conscious and aware and knew what was happening although I had no control. I used to work at an amusement park in my teenage years. One of the rides had a catwalk that went right through a swirling circular tunnel. That is the best way to describe what was happening to me. I felt as if I was being pulled through a tunnel or canal of some sort. I didn't see it, but I somehow sensed it was round about me. It was a definite passageway.

The interesting thing about this is that I didn't want to go through the tunnel! I was being pulled against my will and I didn't have the strength to resist. I did try to resist, but no matter how I fought it, I was still pulled through. I felt powerless, helpless, and out of control. I instinctively knew that the imminence of a meeting with God was on the other side and I shrunk from facing that. Strangely enough what was pulling me through that passageway was my faith! I remember thinking, "Oh no, I believe!" I said "Oh no" because I didn't want to be in this place being pulled out of control. I knew that for months prior I had been believing and seeking, and now that faith became the force that was propelling me toward God. I also said "Oh no" because of the immediacy of what I knew I was about to encounter.

Let me try to explain this more. This passageway is the first thing you encounter at the point of release. When a person's body is old, sick, or damaged by an accident, there is a departure at the moment of death. Your body will eventually wear out and you will need to leave it. Your consciousness, your soul, literally vacates your body and begins its journey toward God. This will occur naturally without our knowing how. It will not take long at all. As I said before, your encounter with divinity will be imminent. You will instinctively know what is about to happen, but there must be this "crossing over" or transition first.

It's important to realize that your soul will never die. That which makes you you, your conscience, your consciousness, your personhood, will be preserved and transformed. Although your body will die, you will live and spend eternity somewhere (heaven or hell).

I believe that this "tunnel" or passageway that I was journeying through is the one that we will all journey through at the moment of our death. When someone "passes away" they go through this cylindrical vortex that is the connection between this life and the next. Philosophically speaking it may be some type of time warp or "worm" or heightened consciousness connector. Its entrance is within our core, our heart. We all have deep within us the opening that leads to the vestibule of eternity.

It's interesting that when we are born into this world, we pass through the tunnel of our mother's womb. No one knows how to be born, it happens naturally. When we are born into the next world, we will all journey through another tunnel. Don't worry about not knowing the way. You will go through it instinctively and naturally. It is much like passing through a revolving door. There is one reality on one side and a very different one on the other side. The common saying, "There is light at the end of the tunnel" is precisely true.

I vividly remember that I fought going through that tunnel. I am used to being in control and fear the loss of control. That is exactly what I experienced then: the complete loss of control. I didn't know where I was, where I was going or what was going to happen to me. In some ways it was like the take-off roll of an airplane. There was no turning back and no way out. I had to surrender to what was occurring to me. I hated the feeling of being out of control, but I didn't have the strength to resist because I was drawn down that passageway by a power much greater than myself. In a way the pull was like the force of gravity. It was impossible to resist.

I know now that God himself was summoning me. Jesus himself said, "No one can come to me unless the Father who sent me *draws* him." (Jn. 6:44) The obvious meaning of this verse is that God will attract people to salvation in Jesus. I found it coming true literally as I was drawn like a magnet to Jesus.

This portal to eternity is a place that transcends time. I remember thinking that it was so peaceful and slow there that it somehow made time, as we know it, stand still or stall. Time is motion, and although I was moving, the realm I was in was beyond time. It's interesting but when talking about the attributes of the Holy Spirit the author of Wisdom states, "For Wisdom is *more mobile than any motion*; because of her pureness she pervades and penetrates all things." (Wis. 7:24) Perhaps that's why the resurrected Jesus was able to enter rooms even though doors were shut and locked. (Jn. 20:19)

STOPWATCH

I watched a movie once where the main character had the power to freeze time by snapping his fingers. When he snapped his fingers all the other people in the movie were at a standstill. As they stood frozen, he walked around and got something to eat. Each character was stopped in the act of talking, gesticulating, or laughing. They looked like wax figures. After getting something to eat he snapped his fingers and everyone resumed what they were doing at the moment they had been frozen. The main character was able to skirt time, yet no time passed during his meal. When we talk about God being transcendent, it means that he is beyond time, mysteriously above it, somehow apart from it, yet he can enter into it.

One way of grasping the concept of time before God is this: imagine placing a ruler before God's face, plotted with every second of time from the dawn of creation until the end of the world. God himself transcends it so that time is stopped before him. He can view it all at once. He can look at the ruler from beginning to end, able at the beginning to foretell the end, able at the beginning to see the end. Time goes at its set pace but God transcends it. Although God stands beside it he can also enter time.

As I went through my experience, I made a mental footnote to myself that everything on earth *seems* so safe and secure. Things are definitely not what they seem. What I mean is that when we think or act or live we feel like we are the only ones present. But just beneath the surface of our thoughts and consciousness, there is a whole new transcendent reality. We live on the tip of the iceberg, as it were. God is within and he is aware of every little detail of our lives. Every thought, motive, action and behavior is under his scrutiny. Somehow God has created a world where it *seems* like we are alone and no one knows our thinking. The way God has ingeniously designed the world, faith and doubt, virtue and vice, love and selfishness can play their roles. A child sure that he is being watched will most likely behave his best, but one unaware of being observed will allow his true self to come to the fore.

I am sure of this: we are never alone. Psalm 139:2 says it best. "You know when I sit down and when I rise up; you discern my thoughts from afar." This "afar" doesn't mean a long distance necessarily, it means beyond time. I believe it was St. Augustine who wisely wrote that God is closer to us than we are to ourselves.

PRAYER IS THE OPENING DOOR

I love to pray contemplatively. The experiences that I am writing about here cause a yearning within me to be that close to God again. Centering prayer brings me into a depth relationship with God. Paul tells us, "set your mind on the things that are above." (Col. 3:2) In the heights of centering prayer, I believe we are able to meet God at this portal. During the Jubilee year 2000, the theme was to "open wide the doors to Christ." This door is at the center of our being, in our heart. "Teach me wisdom in my secret heart." (Ps. 51:6)

Remember what Jesus said, "Behold I stand at the door and knock; if any one hears my voice and opens the door, I will come in to him and eat with him and he with me." (Rev. 3:20) "Behold, the judge is standing at the doors." (Jas. 5:9) I believe that the door talked about in these two verses is the portal to eternity residing in our heart. Few ever find it in this life. Most don't even know it exists and live oblivious to it. Opening that door takes work and discipline and grace. Usually we are far from it, unaware and living in sensuality and carnality. But if we can slow down and get centered, we can begin to transcend time itself and enter the place of rest, God's glorious presence within us.

In the year 2002 the Cathedral of Our Lady of the Angels in Los Angeles was completed at a cost of some $200 million. The cathedral was the work of Jose Rafael Moneo, the great Spanish architect. In many ways the cathedral's asymmetrical and angular shapes were a sharp deviation from conventional church design. Moneo has said that he wanted his design "to offer a space where people feel more able to isolate themselves from daily life." In building a cathedral that has a monastic feel, Moneo rightly seems to be telling us that it is better to look for truth *within* ourselves than to look for it outside of us.

I used to watch the program *Star Trek* on television. It always began with the intro: "Space, the final frontier." I disagree. It is not going outside of ourselves that constitutes the final frontier. The Hubble Telescope won't reveal to us the secrets and answers to the universe. The answers we seek can only be found by looking within. It is a heightened state of consciousness that will reveal the eternal truths we seek. I believe that going within, to our center, and transcendently discovering God and our true selves constitutes "the final frontier."

THE FRONTIER OF DEATH

People are journeying through this portal, this passageway, every day when they die. It is as natural an occurrence as being born. Religious life has helped me to view death from a whole new perspective. Many of the men I have met and lived with as a Passionist have passed to the Lord already. While we mourn their loss, we celebrate their passing! It has blessed me to know there is a constant parade of Passionists who enter eternity. As I write this, four of our priests have died in the past month. Death is an appointment that tens of thousands have every day. Some die of natural causes while others die from accidents or other traumas. When I read the paper today I couldn't help notice the news: Ann Landers died, a 33-year-old major league pitcher died in his sleep, others died from accidents. Perhaps you are aware of a friend or relative or someone in the news who just passed. There is a constant stream of people entering the passageway all the time. Billions from previous generations have preceded us. One day we will pass through too. It's important to remember that death is not the cessation of life, but a new beginning!

THE ULTIMATE SURRENDER

My dad died suddenly on the night of October 23, 2000, at the age of 76. When he went to bed that night, we had no idea that he would not wake up. He suffered a massive stroke. That morning when the doctor informed us that he had in fact passed away, he looked at me and said something interesting. "There was no death struggle," he informed me. Dad had spent his entire life surrendering to suffering, people and circumstances. He had given his life to God over and over again by being a husband and a father. All this was a preparation for the final letting go, his death. He surrendered well in life and didn't struggle in his ultimate letting go.

I believe that we will die as we have lived. If you fight life, continually grasp for control and live independently of God, you will struggle in death. If you surrender to God and to life, trust in God, and grow old gracefully, your death will be the final surrender among many previous ones in your life. Our sufferings, no matter what form they take, are meant to teach us that we are not in control and to surrender to the one who has control. If we abandon ourselves well now, we will embrace death trustingly later.

For some reason, many are called to a deep suffering toward the end of their life. Not everyone passes immediately like my dad did. Dying can be a long and drawn out process, including hospital stays, chemotherapy, machines or drugs. Many have to endure years of cancer, Alzheimer's, strokes and other debilitating diseases. The suffering can be terrible and devastating. Yet, in the midst of it, one is always faced with a choice: surrender to God in the trials or resist and be bitter. The process of dying itself is a call to abandon yourself to God in the struggle. No one on earth will understand the benefit or the difficulty of your daily wrestling, but God will be garnering growth and grace in you. God does have an ultimate purpose and he stores your every tear in his bottle. (Ps. 56:8)

I believe that most people who do not accept the Gospel and give their lives to Christ are prideful controlling people who are not willing to die to self. If we surrender and die to self now, death will be but the final surrender. We will be ready for that moment of letting go. I've met some people who are physically blind and handle it very well. Their faith in God and daily surrender to him is admirable. Others suffer with lesser trials and are bitter about life. Sometimes it is the blind who teach us to see.

The Gospel of John has a unique Passion account. John's Gospel has been called the maverick gospel because it stands alone in its presentation of Jesus and draws upon material that the other three gospels do not include. The moment of Jesus' death is one instance. In

Mark's Gospel, for example, Jesus dies, fully human, with a loud, wordless scream. (Mk. 15:37) In contrast, John's account has Jesus surrendering his spirit to God at the moment of his death. (Jn. 19:30) He gives his spirit back to the one who gave it to him in the first place. Jesus made it clear in John 10:18, "No one takes my life from me, but *I lay it down* of my own accord." In other words, throughout his life he was surrendering to God's will. His final and greatest surrender was at the moment of his death. He yielded his spirit up to God. He recklessly abandoned control. John made the point that Jesus died as he lived: humble, surrendered, abandoned and yielded to God.

I believe we have an inherent desire to grasp for control. Control is a blessing and a curse. The ability to regulate, manage and exercise authority over life and events can enable a person to go far. Leaders, owners, and people with a vision all thrive on being in control. However, the need for control can actually lead to a loss of control. In some ways life is like Jello. We can never really grab hold of it completely in the way we would like. There are always unpredictable occurrences and people that we cannot control. When some people face these situations they can't control, they find their life unmanageable. Some turn to drinking and drugs as a way of escape and coping. Many in the Twelve Step Programs are people who feel out of control. There is a saying: A man takes a drink, a drink takes a man. Drinking or any addiction begins as a toehold, continues as a foothold and stronghold and turns into a stranglehold. Ironically, the way to regain control is through the process of surrender.

Pride is the epitome of grasping for control. It is self-reliance and wanting your own way all the time. Humility surrenders gracefully to the changes and uncertainties of life. We are told that what set Jesus apart was that he emptied himself and humbled himself even unto death on a Cross. (Phil. 2:7-8)

Life is always presenting us with opportunities to surrender. No matter what your vocation is, God will work through people, circumstances and life events to bring you to new levels of growth and sanctification. God isn't necessarily trying to remove all of the control from our lives, but rather to keep us in balance. Recently, after living in Sacramento for ten years, I was asked by my superiors to move to Houston. I have lived in Houston for a year now. The residence is different, the people are different and I long for things the way they were. I find myself getting nostalgic and romanticizing the past. Of course the past wasn't as great as I remember it to be, but we do have a way of making it better in our memory than it actually was. The people of Israel did the same thing when they left Egypt. As bad as Egypt was, they remembered it with fondness. "We remember the fish we ate in Egypt for nothing, the cucumbers, the melons, the leeks, the onions, and the garlic." (Num. 11:5) What they forgot was the slavery and harsh treatment. Beware of romanticizing the past. Your aggrandized nostalgia will make it that much harder to adapt to new situations.

One source of struggle with my move to Houston is my perceived loss of freedom here. Back in Sacramento, I used to be able to go to the kitchen in our residence, get breakfast and park myself in front of the T.V. while I ate. I am not a morning person and I like my private space, especially early in the morning. When I moved to Houston, I kept that same routine. Apparently it was upsetting to some in the community who want us all to eat breakfast together. My superior talked to me about it and it was agreed that we would all eat in the common room and share breakfast together with one another. At first I resisted this arrangement. I wanted to eat breakfast by myself as I always used to. But I have been surrendering to the process and have actually found it beneficial. I am developing deeper relationships with the people I live with. Now we talk more about the things that are happening each day. I have found that it is not that hard to eat in common. My surrender has led to growth. Although it was hard at first, it is getting easier. Relationships bring opportunities for surrender and adjustment. People are in our lives for a reason.

In my new situation in Houston, I try to receive each new day with thanksgiving and not look back to what was. I have learned that God still has a dream for my life. Just because situations, circumstances and people have changed, it doesn't mean that God's good plan for my life has been thwarted. God wills a glorious destiny for us. We can only receive it if we let go of the past and embrace what is and what will be. "Behold, the former things have come to pass, and new things I now declare." (Is. 42:9) God has new things for us! Don't miss his plan for your life by staying in grief about the way things used to be. Don't stay stuck by romanticizing the past. This is a new day and God has fresh *new things* in store for you. Look to the future with hope.

I meet people all the time who are being called upon to surrender to the process of life. My best friends, who help me distribute my books and tapes, have known for a while that their house is way too big for them. All four of their children have moved out and they are wrestling with the empty nest syndrome. Since they need money and do not spend a lot of time at home anymore, they made the choice to sell the house and move to another state. Although they made this decision themselves, it doesn't make the pain of leaving a place they love any easier. They have both grown to love the space where their children grew up and much of their marriage was lived. In their struggles with adapting to the move, they are turning to God and his grace to cope with the pain. They believe in God's plan for their future. They are learning the grace as well as the pain of surrender.

My mother lost my dad some two years ago. After being married for 54 years and knowing no one else but my father, suddenly she was almost 80 years old and alone. Not only did she lose the love of her life, now she is also dealing with old age and health issues. Every day she has to turn to God and surrender. There are hundreds of thousands of widows and widowers in the same boat. The mother of a good friend of mine just moved into an assisted living facility. She lost her husband three years ago and now she was forced to move from her house of many years. Life and growing older require coping and deep surrender. One can deny the facts of life and resist, or surrender to the process. The journey of life is a process pregnant with growth through the presence of God.

There are countless situations that require our surrender. People talk to me all the time about their children. Some have left the faith, others marry people their parents don't like, still others are unemployed and cause great heartache. People cannot control their children. Neither can we control our Church. The Church certainly isn't perfect. Recently we have gone through the priest sex scandal. Many of the priests and the people are confused and disillusioned. The sex scandal, the aging priesthood, the lack of vocations, and the choices of other people are beyond our complete control. In addition we must deal with terrorism, pollution, injustice, poverty, overcrowding, accidents, earthquakes, fires, murders, theft, and noise.

QUIET PLEASE

I've been told that one of the worst things about being incarcerated is the noise. There are doors being slammed constantly, people laughing and shouting and loud bangs intermittently. People scream just to be noticed. I am very sensitive to noise and it has been a concern for me wherever I live. I treasure silence and living in community can be a problem. If we try to get together and pray quietly in common, someone will cough or there will be air conditioners going or other things that distract me. I live in a place where eight of us live in close quarters. I often hear doors being opened and slammed, music, alarm clocks, phones ringing and the usual household noises. In the morning crows caw early and loudly. Dogs will get stirred up and bark at night. Airplanes fly over. Lawn maintenance workers mow and blow various yards all day on Friday. The air conditioner, essential in our Houston climate, makes a constant whirr. Lately, everywhere I go to preach a mission has some kind of construction going on. There are the sounds of hammering, sawing, beeping trucks backing, mowing, blowing and air conditioners.

When I fly on planes it seems I always sit next to someone who is sniffling, clearing their throat, popping gum or coughing every 20 seconds. Often people behind me strike up and carry on a conversation that I cannot avoid overhearing. Those traveling alone are talking on cell phones. Most places have helicopters flying around, traffic, and sirens. When I go on my yearly retreat, I always try to get the end room and crave a place that will be quiet.

At least once a year I want silence! I read an article when I first entered religious life called "Noisy Contemplation." Little did I know how prophetic that was! The trick of being able to pray is to do it in the midst of noise.

We cannot leave this noise pollution. I have tried to ignore it. Fighting it does no good. I am growing in my ability to shut it out. I have hypersensitive hearing. I believe God allows me to have "rabbit ears" to remind me that I am not in control. I used to think I deserved silence. Now I realize that no one is spared life's disturbances. Coping with noise is part of the great surrender of life for me.

For some reason we come into life with the illusion that we can run our own life just the way we want. That simply is not true. We can't have it exactly the way we want it. Frank Sinatra sang "I did it my way," but the reality is that we have to be flexible and adaptable and surrender to what is. We must surrender to imperfect relationships, health problems, growing older, losing friends, losing hair, loneliness, trials, adversities, and various other difficulties. Imperfections and irritations are part and parcel of life. I'm not saying that we must passively "take" all of this. For example, if loneliness is a problem, be proactive and take responsibility for your loneliness by getting involved in the community. Make your marriage more amicable by going to counseling. Take care of yourself physically and perhaps you will prevent future problems. But we must understand that we don't live in a perfect world. There is no perfect marriage, church, job, hometown, or body.

STOP RUNNING

Coping with life and the circumstances that life brings can make us bitter or better. I really believe that

God purposely puts us in places that require us to grow. I remember once struggling with the relationships I had in community and I wanted out. I thought, "If I just get out of here things will be better and I will be happy." Then I sensed God speaking to me. He said, "Cedric, bloom where you are planted. It will be the same wherever you go. Try to be happy where I have you." I have determined that no matter where I go or what I do there will be difficulties. What matters is how you handle what you have on your plate *now*. Running away won't help things and could even delay your growth process. Whenever people in the Bible ran from God's will, God always made them come back and face it. A perfect example of that was the prophet Jonah. He was told to preach to the people of Nineveh but instead Jonah ran the other way. A trip to the belly of a whale and a seaweed supper changed all that. His suffering broke his pride and forced his surrender to God's will. Hardships have a way of making us much more flexible and manageable.

The difference between the words bitter and better is the small letter "I". It is our selfishness and our narcissism that must die. When we surrender, a little part of us dies so that our true self can emerge. One of my overriding goals for my life is to become a person of love. "Be perfect as your heavenly Father is perfect," Jesus taught. (Mt. 5:48) The word perfection in the Greek has the implication of becoming whole and complete. It is the end we must strive for. We achieve this goal by loving others.

One time I was struggling with community and stewed in self-pity and had thoughts of leaving. As I mulled over my situation I sensed God telling me, "Cedric, the people in this community are the road I have put you on to transform you into a person of love." I discovered that I must bloom where I am planted and look for the fulfillment of God's will for my life right where I live. It is tempting to think about what life could be like somewhere else. It is easy to reason, "If only I was married (or not married!), or had more money, or wasn't sick . . ." Look at your life right now. Most likely where God has you now is where he is calling you to bloom, love and find contentment.

It is so easy for me to get negative, murmur, grumble, find fault and complain. I find myself in my room or taking a walk or sitting and thinking, "I hate this. I want things to be different. I can't believe this." An attitude like that delays the process of growth and begets further cynicism, negativity and unhappiness. Rather "give thanks in *all circumstances*; for this is the will of God in Christ Jesus for you." (1 Thes. 5:18) If you grumble about your problems all the time you are not growing, you are grasping for control. God has been speaking to me about offering him the sacrifice of praise. That means that I am to thank God in the midst of trials. It is a sacrifice because it is *hard* to offer God praise in the difficulties of life, but this is part of the surrender process too. In any sacrifice there is surrender. You must see God's will in the minutest parts of your life. As you do, give God praise. Gratitude will open up your heart to a new flow of life and peace.

Are you dealing with difficult people? Do you have health problems and suffer? Have you recently lost a loved one? Is there someone you need to forgive? Are you lonely and discouraged? God is calling everyone to die to self and to live according to his will. Don't struggle, deny or resist. Surrender! Life is a process of abandonment and letting go. Some things you can change, and I pray you have the courage to do so. Most things you cannot change. I pray you have the fortitude to accept these and surrender. I invite you to pray:

Lord, I need your help.
People and circumstances are
out of my control.
I want to learn from life and grow.
I surrender myself to you.
Help me to change what I can.
I pray for contentment in the situations
I can't change.
I want to bloom where I am planted.
I love you Lord.
Amen.

We are all heading toward the death experience. It will be an encounter with ultimate powerlessness and loss of control, yet it is a healing, an encounter with grace. Are you ready for the final surrender? We prepare ourselves well by surrendering ourselves to God now. We surrender by allowing God's power to take control of our lives in the midst of our hard times. We must be adaptable and flexible when it comes to the negative people and circumstances of our lives. We ready ourselves for death by allowing God's will for us to transform us now.

5
GOD IS LIGHT AND LOVE

"Death is not extinguishing the light; it is putting out the lamp because the Dawn has come." –Tagore

Before I knew it, I was at the end of the tunnel. Suddenly, I found myself in the presence of God himself. Before I say anything else, I want to convey that I knew within me that I had been there before. It wasn't a vague recollection, it was a vivid memory realized. When we are born into this world, we "forget" where we have come from. The reason is so that faith will play her role. I have read similar thoughts from Eastern spiritual masters who talk about life in this world as a "forgetting." From my experience I know they are right.

On the day we die, we will know as we are known. Apparently Jesus, through his prayer and the revelations God gave him, had broken through and remembered where he had come from. He taught, "I know where I've come from and where I am going." (Jn. 8:14) At the Last Supper Jesus knew that he had come from God and was going to God. (Jn. 13:3) Whether we remember or not, we have all come from God and we will all one day return to God. God loans us our souls for a little while to see what type of life we will lead. We must justify our souls now because all of a sudden the long journey of life will end. Then we will view the deeds of our time of "forgetting" on earth, remembering where we came from. There will be great shame for those who have not proved worthy of their soul, as well as great joy for those who lived in faith.

GOD

One day every person who has ever lived will stand before God. What I encountered when I stood before him was glorious and magnificent. I wasn't allowed to see a form, but what I did see was light. (I literally saw the light!) It was as if I were looking at the sun with my eyes closed, yet even brighter. It was a pure, luminescent light. Psalm 104:1-2 tells us the truth that "God is clothed with honor and majesty, and covers himself with light as with a garment." I didn't just see the light, the brightness embraced me. I was touched, warmed and blessed by this divine light which penetrated me.

In addition to the brightness, there was incredible glory. God's glory is a constant theme in the Bible. David prayed seeking God and remembered how he had seen God's power and glory in the sanctuary. (Ps. 63:1-2) God is the king of glory (Ps. 24:8, 10) The word glory in Hebrew has the meaning of honor, adornment, beauty and majesty. It is an attribute of God's magnificence because of who he is and what he has done. The prophet Ezekiel tried to describe his vision of God's glory. "Like the appearance of the rainbow that is in the cloud on the day of rain, so was the appearance of the brightness round about the throne. Such was the appearance of the likeness of the glory of the Lord." (Ez. 1:28) This same rainbow is spoken of in the majestic chapter 4 of the book of Revelation. "And he who sat upon the throne appeared like jasper and carnelian, and round the throne was a rainbow that looked like an emerald." (Rev. 4:3)

God's glory is not just something I observed, it was an electricity and ecstasy that I *felt*. It was a rhythmic powerful surge that ran all through me. I could even see it. With light as the background, I could actually see horizontal lines consistently and constantly running upwards through me! The only example I can think of that describes this is when the T.V. is not adjusted correctly and the dark horizontal lines run upwards constantly. God is immensely glorious and the waves of glory were constant and powerful. There was nothing painful; rather, the glory was the source of bliss and ecstasy. It is pure pleasure to be in the presence of God. I was experiencing the pleasure all humans seek all our lives, the joy for which we were made. This is the ultimate pleasure for which we long. What I experienced was a portion of the beatific vision for which we are all heading. "For this slight momentary affliction is preparing for us an eternal weight of glory beyond all comparison." (2 Cor. 4:17) God's honor became my honor. The Lord was my shepherd and I did not want! The triumphant victory and honor given Jesus because of the Cross was bestowed upon me too. You must prepare yourself for the moment of death because every person will either receive the glory of honor or wither away in shame before God.

Actually, God *wants* to share his glory with everyone. He has an inexhaustible supply for all. Psalm 8:5 tells us that God has already crowned humans with glory and honor. One of my favorite verses in the Bible is Romans 8:29-30, which reveals that God has predestined, called and justified us so that we can share in his glory. I wrote about God's glory in my second book, *Glorious Holy Spirit.* I came to understand through my near-death experiences that the same glory I encountered in God's presence was now mine to enjoy *daily* through the person and presence of the Holy Spirit who dwells in me. I sense this glory to a lesser degree now, but nevertheless it is still present. The feeling causes goose bumps, chills up and down the spine and other sensations of pleasure.

One of the greatest delights of heaven will be that we will share in God's glory forever. The prophet Isaiah tells us in 43:7 that we were created for God's glory! God wants us to enjoy this pleasure and rapture. It is the glory of love. He wants us to delight in the honor, majesty and victory that were won at Calvary. Not only that, we will be rapt in our attention of God as we worship. Finally, we will appreciate and know that we have been saved and redeemed by the Lamb. Isaiah gives us a glimpse of heaven when he writes, "On that day we will say, 'This is our God for whom we have waited. Let us rejoice and be glad in his salvation.'" (Is. 25:9) We have a tremendous inheritance of bliss awaiting us and can share in the foretaste now through the Holy Spirit.

The word ecstasy literally means to be beside oneself. As I stood before God embraced by light, clothed in glory, and reveling in the bliss, I noticed that I couldn't really think the way I usually do. What I mean is that here on earth we can choose to think certain thoughts. For example, if I want to remember a golf game I played recently, it is easy to do. I simply choose to think about it and I remember. Or if I want to engage in self-reflection and notice how I feel, I am able to do so simply by thinking about it. But when I was in God's presence, I remember that I was so full of God and his peace that it seemed like I had lost the ability to choose my thoughts. I know that many are distressed because of distracting thoughts and evil imaginings that pop into our minds when we don't want them to. That will not occur in God's presence. I was possessed by God! The writer of the letter to the Ephesians prayed a beautiful prayer, hoping that we would know the love of Christ that surpasses all knowledge and "be filled with all the fullness of God." (Eph. 3:19) Even now to a lesser degree, when we are filled with the Holy Spirit or allow ourselves to be filled with the fullness of God, we allow God to take control of our minds, decisions and emotions.

Don't let being possessed by God scare you. In this world, being human involves many negative thoughts such as fears, anxieties, bad memories, regrets, stress, sins, etc. The battlefield with the devil is our minds. Many deal with depression, despair, loneliness and panic. We won't be able to think of such things anymore. Instead, we will be "beside ourselves" and be renewed in our minds. We will think *God's* thoughts and know his ways. We will be totally his. We will still be a distinct soul and our own unique self, but very God-like. Jesus said that in the afterlife, we would be like angels of God. (Mt. 22:30) *Our* faces will shine like the sun in our Father's kingdom. (Mt. 13:43) Heaven will be life the way it was meant to be. We will be joyful, peaceful, and imbued with delight and honor. We were made for honor. We were made for glory. God will complete and fulfill us.

GOD IS LOVE (1 JN 4:8)

On my pilgrimage to the shrines of Italy, our journey of faith took us to places such as Milan, Florence, Assisi, Sienna, Padua, and Rome. One of the towns we visited was called Lanciano. It is a small town in east-central Italy.

Back in the year 800 a priest was presiding at the Eucharist. He had doubts about the real presence of Jesus at Mass. As he was celebrating, suddenly the bread turned into flesh and the wine changed into real blood! He was amazed by this miracle, and it led him to deep faith in the real presence of Jesus in the Eucharist. This has been one of the central tenets of the Catholic faith for centuries. Jesus *is* really present in the auspices of bread and wine.

The host and blood from that miracle were safeguarded and protected and are available for viewing today. The flesh is about the size of a three-inch round host. The blood, coagulated into five irregular globules, is kept in a cup. About 30 years ago two scientists, professors from the University of Sienna, conducted experiments on the elements. The analyses were conducted with absolute scientific precision and they were documented with a series of microscopic photographs. Their findings were quite interesting.

They discovered that not only was the bread-host turned to human flesh, but also the flesh was heart tissue. I don't know what that does for you, but for me, that makes perfect sense. In the Eucharist God is giving his very heart, his self, for us in love. I know this as a priest. When I preside at the Eucharist and come to the place of Jesus' words, "This is my body which will be given up for you," I always feel something go out of my heart. In that moment, all my sacrifice for God and for people as a priest unites to the love of God given in Jesus' sacrifice of his body. It is an emotion, an emanation of love that flows from me at that Eucharistic moment. I feel it. I know it to be true. God is giving his heart to us because God is love.

On Valentine's Day, lovers always send valentines in the shape of hearts or with hearts on them. The heart is the symbol of love. For God to give us his heart means that he gave us the center of who he is. His heart is giving and forgiving. In a way, Eucharist is the ultimate valentine.

The scientists examined the blood, too. They found that it was the most rare type, type AB. Before I studied blood types, I figured that AB would probably be the universal donor, since Jesus was always giving to people.

As I studied, what I found is that AB is not the universal donor as I suspected, but the universal *receiver!* In other words, if you have type AB blood, you can safely receive a transfusion from someone with any other blood type.

That didn't make sense to me for a while. Then I prayed about this and came to understand. Jesus was always *receiving* people. Often it was sinners, tax collectors, or prostitutes that he attracted. He bore a lot of flack from the religious leaders of his day because he associated with outcasts. One day he sat at table with many tax collectors and sinners. When the Pharisees saw this, they said to his disciples, "Why does your teacher eat with tax collectors and sinners?" When Jesus heard them he replied, "Those who are well have no need of a doctor, but those who are sick." (Mt. 9:10-13) Jesus is always inviting us, "Come to me." (Mt. 11:28) In John's Gospel, when Jesus was discoursing about the Eucharist, he made this beautiful comment, "All that the Father gives me will come to me; and the one who comes to me I will not cast out." (Jn. 6:37) Jesus is the universal receiver. He loves you. Come to him as you are and he will accept you.

Last spring I was in Worcester, Massachusetts preaching at a graduation Mass at Venerini Academy. My cousin was graduating from the eighth grade and I had been asked by his mother to preside over the graduation. A mosaic was visible, right on the altar, of a bird wounding itself and bleeding. Beside and beneath the bird were three little chicks drinking the blood. In the upper room in Jerusalem, the traditional place of the Last Supper, I saw a similar carving on one of the capitals. Why this particular mosaic on an altar and this carving at the place of the Last Supper?

Tradition has it that the mother pelican will actually wound herself and feed her young with her blood so they won't go hungry. The pelican appears on various altars, churches and at the site of the Last Supper because it is an appropriate image to show God's love for us. In the person of Jesus, God has actually been wounded and he feeds us with his shed blood out of love for us. When we eat his body and drink his blood, we participate in the love God has for us. In fact, one of the earliest terms for Eucharist was an agape feast. Agape is one of the Greek words for love. This particular word for love has the meaning of *God's* love which is unmerited, undeserved and unconditional. The pelican image is related to Eucharist because God's love is also sacrificial. Jesus actually gave himself to God and to the world on the Cross. We re-present that one sacrifice every time we celebrate Mass. We celebrate God's awesome sacrificial, unconditional, profound love for each of us.

Because of my experience in God's presence, I know that words alone don't suffice for talking about God and God's love. Perhaps poems or songs could lift our thoughts to this noble realm better than my mere words. How can I talk of God? How can I *not* talk of God! He knows the end from the beginning and the beginning from the end. He does not age or fit into space. God holds the wealth and breadth and depths of human experience in his heart. He is full of wisdom, majesty and grandeur. Everything that is beautiful, lovely and gracious flows from his heart. He has graciously called all of us into being from nothing. God walks with us through thick and thin, delivers us, and saves us. God fills the universe with his majesty. God is simply astounding!

I have written about God's love in many of my other books. For example in my book *Glorious Holy Spirit,* I talk about how "God's love has been poured into our hearts

through the Holy Spirit which has been given to us."
(Rom. 5:5) I usually talk about God's love in terms of
stories I've found so that in some way we can try to grasp
his love for us. The story of Lanciano is a love story. The
Eucharist is God's love story. God sends his son who
sacrifices himself for us out of love. I write and preach
about God's love so often because more than anything
else, what I encountered when I was ushered into God's
presence was love.

THE POWER OF LOVE

God's love for me was intensely personal. I sensed
that I was known and loved even before I was born into
this world. His love was unconditional. God's care and
affection for me were not conditioned on my goodness;
rather, there was such powerful, pulsating, goodness
radiating from God that it was overwhelming. The love
I am talking about was an ardent affection. It was not just
some philosophical, intellectual, rational *idea* of love. God
cares for us. His love was totally self-giving. Everyone is
loved unconditionally whether he or she is aware of it or
not. If we could but for a moment appreciate having been
given life out of complete nonexistence, we would begin
to recognize the sheer depth of God's love.

I realized that not only did God love me; he was *in
love* with me. What I mean is that he knew me through
and through and still had his heart set upon me. Much
like newlyweds who are about to consummate their
vows on their wedding night, there was profound self-
communication and self-sharing. I understood who I really
was in this love! God was being vulnerable and intimate
with me. There were no more secrets. I remember being
amazed at how vulnerable and intimate God wanted to
be. I was invited in to the "Holy of Holies."

I remember thinking, "He loves me so much it is scary." Scary is a strange adjective to use about love, I know, but I was overwhelmed with the intensity and passion of God's love. Agape love was displayed through Jesus in his willingness to be tortured on the Cross. True love is willing to suffer. This love is deep, committed and unwavering. God is not afraid of commitment. In fact, his love is all about commitment. I love this verse from the prophet Isaiah, "Can a woman forget her sucking child, that she should have no compassion on the son of her womb? Even these may forget, yet *I will not forget you.* Behold, I have carved you on the palms of my hands." (Is. 49:15-16)

God is extremely devoted to us and he will remain faithful and never falter. There is such depth and determination in God's passionate love. The force and strength of God's love was overwhelming, so encompassing that I lost myself in it. I was absorbed in God's love and I have come to understand these beautiful words of Paul, "I am sure that neither death . . . nor anything else in all creation, will be able to separate us from the love of God in Christ Jesus our Lord." (Rom. 8:38-39) Truly God's love is even more powerful than death itself!

Paul talked about the scope of the glorious power of God's love when he wrote, "May God give you the ability to know what is the immeasurable greatness of his power in us who believe." (Eph. 1:17-18) Some time back I had friends of mine visit from Michigan. We toured around Houston and one of the places I took them was to N.A.S.A.'s mission control. It was a fascinating visit. We learned about the space station and toured museums and were educated about space travel.

During our visit, something special occurred. We just happened to be there the day that five shuttle astronauts were present to brief the crowd about their flight. These particular astronauts had just returned from their mission to repair the Hubble Telescope. Of course, the Hubble Telescope has been in space for many years and has sent back fantastic pictures of the universe. One of the repairs they made was to the lens itself. They inserted a new lens that would enable the telescope to view distant worlds ten times better than it already did. As I write this, the pictures that Hubble is transmitting back to earth, in the words of one scientist, are "stunning." We are seeing galaxies hundreds of thousands of light-years away. We are able to view stars being born and collapsing. Scientists are surmising that the universe is now older than they first thought. The expanse out there is beyond our ability to grasp no matter how powerful our eye in the sky is.

Our galaxy is called the Milky Way. The speed that light travels is 186,000 miles per second. In one minute, light travels over 11 million miles. Imagine how far light would travel in one year. Now, picture this: our galaxy is some *100,000* light years across. Astronomers tell us that our galaxy is not a large one compared to some of the others out there. The Hubble Telescope has shown us there are some 125 *billion* galaxies in the universe. Wow!

The sights of Hubble and the size of our universe give us an idea of the corresponding love and greatness of God. (Wis. 13:5) God's love is unparalleled, unbounded, and everlasting. There is no beginning or end to it. It is powerful, creative, expansive and life-giving. When I think about the universe and the over six billion people on earth, I begin to get some glimpse into the power and majesty of God's love. It was this power that I felt coursing through me and utterly amazing me.

I know that because of God's love I will always be cared for, thought about, sought after, encouraged and graced. God is able at one and the same time to be aware of all people at once. We never need to believe the lie that we are alone or that our lives don't matter. The wonderful truth that God is always with us means we need not feel desolate, abandoned or forsaken. God will never fail us. God says, "You are precious in my eyes, honored, and I love you." (Is. 43:4) How can the burning, passionate, wooing love of God not capture and melt even the hardest of hearts?

JESUS: THE CURE FOR THE INSECURE

At some point in life everyone must come to the point of self-acceptance. This is hard to do because we are all acutely aware of our misshapen bodies, persistent faults, wayward thoughts and impure motivations. We are all limited and lacking in certain gifts. We may not like the way we look. For most of my life I have struggled with a low self-image, feelings of inadequacy, low self-esteem and perfectionism. I know that I am not the most intelligent, the best looking, or perfectly holy. I am not the best writer, preacher or athlete. My awareness of my faults led me to grow in self-hate and self-rejection. It caused anger, fear and a lot of inner sadness.

I still have to deal with all these issues in myself. I don't deny them, but recognize this in me and face it. I want to share that it is God's love that has pushed me over the edge in terms of self-acceptance. I have come to realize that I am lovable. I am lovable not because I am the best at anything, but because God is in love with me. God's love has led me to a deep, basic, inner decision of self-acceptance. I can now forgive myself for the wrongs

I have committed, laugh at myself when I mess up, and not beat myself up when I do not perform perfectly. Those who sin by letting themselves go physically and then giving up on their dreams are manifesting self-rejection. Instead of sabotaging myself, God's love has led me to befriend myself. I encourage myself, discipline myself and set goals. I strive to bear fruit and be a blessing to people. I am much more gentle with myself when I yield to fear or failure. Although I try not to beat myself up and berate myself when I fail, I still remain determined and try not to compromise. These are the hallmarks of self-acceptance and personal growth.

God knows me through and through and *still* loves me. That helps me and changes my view of myself. In the words of the *Desiderata*, "I am a child of the universe and I have a *right to be here*." I have a right to be here because God himself called me into being. You have a right to be here because God wants you here. God created his one and only universe with you in it. All of us were created for a purpose.

Don't despise yourself or focus on your shortcomings. I was reflecting on my timid shy nature on retreat recently. Sometimes I feel embarrassed about interrupting and disrupting people's lives by my preaching. When I proclaim the Gospel, I boldly gallivant around the sanctuary as I call people to Christ. For some I am too much. Deep inside I tell myself that I am shy and don't like the limelight. As I thought about my timidity, I received a powerful impulse from the Lord who said, "Even though you don't have a need to be noticed, you have *a right* to be noticed." That encouraged me a lot. I don't necessarily want to be before people all the time, but because of God, I have a right to be.

You are more than just okay; the Bible says that you are *very* good. (Gen. 1:31) God will always be in love with you. The devil wants you to reject yourself and will do everything he can to convince you to do so. Receiving, accepting, and experiencing God's love will help you to accept yourself and become more self-secure. Knowing that God approves of you in Christ will help you to approve of yourself. The reality of God's love will bring healing for the scars that life can bring.

WHO DO PEOPLE SAY THAT I AM?

Many of us know we need to work on our self-image. But what about our God-image? One of the truths I feel most called to proclaim is in the area of our God-image. We develop our image of God in a number of ways. The input from parents, priests, T.V., friends, and books mediates a sense of what God is like. God-image is the perception of God that we hold deep within our heart. More important than God's attributes, like being all-powerful or all-knowing, is how we believe God relates to us.

For example, many grew up in a strict, harsh church environment. Maybe you had parents who stressed the rigorous laws of religion. Possibly you had a pastor who was stern or never smiled. What tends to happen in situations like these is that people develop an idea of a God who is demanding and harsh. People will then think, "God never has any fun and doesn't want us to have fun." Or "God wants perfect obedience and anything short deserves punishment." (As you will see later, God does not call us to perfection, but to maturity.) God's laws and rules and regulations are many and no human being can live up to these. The fruit of such thinking is that you always feel like you have failed God. You sense that God is out to get you. Any little suffering that you have in life you can interpret as a punishment because you were not good and perfect. In some sense you see God as the computer in the sky keeping a ledger of all that you have done or not done. You can never measure up and because of that you will be cursed.

The other extreme that people fall into is thinking that God is their buddy. God is a sweet, serendipitous, "anything goes" God because forgiveness abounds no matter what. People who believe this are always talking to God, but to a God of their own imagination and making, not the true God. Some who have been in the Twelve Step Program join what is called the Universalist Church. This church is a very lax, New Age type of religion. It is designed to be ultra-accepting of any lifestyle so that people will be given space to nurse their wounds. Their God is loving, true, but these people disregard the just judgment to come. Rightly, they try to improve their behavior, but in their own way on their own terms. For many adherents of this denomination, truth is relative and not absolute. The challenges and demanding truths of the Gospel are not stressed. A sugar-daddy image of God can be just as dangerous as a strict and harsh one.

Of course what we need is balance. God is a God of tender love, but also a God of justice. God is not watching for your every false move so he can condemn you. He is looking for your growth and wants to develop a personal, intimate relationship with you. He doesn't want to punish you, but he may discipline you because he loves you. (Heb. 12:5-11)

To some degree I had that harsh image of God ingrained in me. I knew if I messed up, God would be there to condemn me. As a teenager I did so many things wrong and committed so many sins. I finally gave up trying to please God and fell away. I was way beyond the limit! But when I encountered God's love, I came to know in the depths of my being that God is *for* me, not against me!

Throughout my life I haven't been able to manage my behavior as I want. In spite of my consternation, I have found that God actually helps me rather than condemning me. Where sin abounds, grace abounds all the more. If I stumble along the way, it is God himself who picks me up. If I fail, it is God who forgives me. When I am weak, it is God who gives me strength. "If God is for us, who can be against?" (Rom. 8:31) An encounter with God's love helped bring major healing to my God-image. God is not the big eye in the sky out to get you. Neither is God the great big teddy bear who says, "Anything goes." God is your father, of profound character, integrity and grace. Through my contact with God's love, I have grown leaps and bounds in my image of God. God's love has brought me a solid God-image and healing.

The New Catholic Catechism echoes the old Baltimore Catechism: we were created to know, love, and serve God in this world and to be happy with him in the next. (*Catechism* #1) This is the reason and purpose for our existence. There ought to be less emphasis on law and servitude and more on love and relationship. Instead of loving God because it is commanded, we need to grow to the point where we fall in love with God.

My primary message as a Catholic priest and evangelist has been and always will be this: God loves you. God is in love with you. No matter what sins you have committed or wrong you have done, God is there for you. God's love is the greatest power in the universe. Believe in his love.

Nothing, not even death, will ever separate you from it. "I am my beloved's and his desire is for me." (Song 7:10) I really believe that Christianity is not so much a religion as a love affair between God and each individual person. Nothing is more intimate, rapturous and thrilling than being loved by God and loving him in return. The question I want you to consider is not how religious you are; rather, what kind of lover are you?

6
THE VOICE OF THE LORD

The fourth Sunday of Easter is also called Good Shepherd Sunday. The Gospel readings for each of the three liturgical years (A, B, and C) stress Jesus as the Good Shepherd. The Gospel for the third year of the three-year cycle includes, "My sheep hear my voice. I know them and they follow me." (Jn.10:27) I love the alternative opening prayer for that Sunday. "*Attune* our minds to the sound of his voice, lead our steps in the path he has shown, that we may know the strength of his outstretched arm and enjoy the light of your presence for ever." That prayer resonates in my heart because that is exactly what I experienced.

My mind was definitely attuned to the sound of God's voice while I was in his presence. However, I only remember two phrases the whole time I was there. The first was, "I will protect you." (The second, "You must justify your soul," I will write about later.) To say that I heard a sound like we humans hear would be incorrect. God's voice was communicated to me via thought. It was a knowing, a sensing, but a definite, clear communication. (These "impulses" can be sensed even now through the Holy Spirit.) The knowing was very distinct and I will remember these communications to me until the day I go before God again.

I stood there bathed in light, ecstatic in glory and full of peace. I vividly remember having the biggest smile on my face that I ever had. There is the fullness of joy in God's presence. I wasn't laughing, but rather I had joyful bliss as the message "I will protect you" resounded in me. The famous Scripture that comes to mind is "The Lord is my shepherd, I shall *not want*." (Ps. 23:1) I also felt an arm on my shoulder and around my neck. I was sure it was the arm of Jesus. Throughout the Scriptures, the arm of the Lord is talked about. Mostly, the arm of the Lord has to do with his salvation power. It also has to do with his tender love. Isaiah 40:10-11 is a good example of both:

> Behold, the Lord God comes with might,
> and his *arm* rules for him;
> behold, his reward is with him,
> and his recompense before him.
> He will feed his flock like a shepherd,
> He will gather the lambs in his *arms,*
> He will carry them in his bosom,
> and gently lead those that are with young.

His word of protection to me first of all meant that he would always be with me. I know that as I journey through the mystery of my life, I am never alone. I know his leading and companionship. Secondly, protection did not mean that I would never suffer, but that I would be protected from losing my soul. His promise of protection meant eternal life. It meant that I was saved. Lastly, for me, it meant that I will always belong to him. I am his possession. I am one of the sheep of his flock. Evil will never take me away from Jesus. These words of Jesus are for you too.

"My sheep hear my voice, and I know them and they follow me; and I give them eternal life, and they shall never perish, and no one shall snatch them out of my hand." (Jn. 10:27-28)

PROVIDENTIAL PROTECTION

Jesus works through circumstances, people, coincidences, and even angels to help his flock. Jesus protects us in many instances. One famous incident happened in the life of Pope John Paul II. Back on May 13, 1981 some 40,000 people were gathered for the weekly Wednesday papal audience in St. Peter's Square. As the Pope traveled through the crowd in the pope-mobile, a trained Turkish assassin shot him at near point-blank range. The Pope should have been killed by the bullet but was mysteriously protected from death. The attending surgeon was worried, but amazed. "I noticed something incredible," he said. "The bullet seemed to zigzag through the abdomen, missing the vital organs. It just missed the aorta, too." The Pope believes that Our Lady of Fatima and the prayers of God's people protected him. "One hand fired the bullet and another hand guided it," he said. God doesn't always protect us from suffering the trials of life, but he brings us through them.

I love the story my dad told me about a mysterious protection he received during his days of service in World War II. When he was 20 years old, he was in the U.S. Navy serving in the South Pacific. He was scheduled for submarine duty that particular day and spent much of the morning packing his belongings and getting ready to leave. As he was in line, duffel bag slung over his shoulder, waiting to board the submarine, he heard over the loudspeaker: "Cedric Pisegna, report to the lieutenant, your orders have been changed." My dad reported to his superior to find that he was to report for shore duty. Eerily, the submarine left dock that day and never returned again.

There are millions of such cases. Perhaps as you review your own life or family history you are aware of the mystery of divine providence and protection. The obvious question about my dad's case is, "What about those who went down in that submarine that day?" Where was God's protection in their lives? That is a question we simply can't answer this side of heaven. Why does God protect in some cases and allow terrible things in other cases? It is a mystery. Even though we don't understand everything, we can still believe that God is our protector. God is watching over us. He is our shepherd and evil will never snatch us out of his hands.

The apostle Paul has always been one of my great inspirations. He journeyed to many places proclaiming Jesus. He founded new churches, built up existing churches, and wrote a good portion of the New Testament. He lived a life of excellence, integrity and discipline. Although the Lord was with him, he still suffered and eventually he was martyred. June 29th is his feast day, shared with St. Peter. The second reading for the feast of Sts. Peter and Paul comes from 2 Timothy. It talks about how Paul had lived a life of fire and passion for Jesus. He had kept the goal before him and lived God's will. I am inspired as I read about Paul's utter confidence in God's protection in his life. Paul was a man who knew that his end was near, but still trusted in God's providence.

> For I am already on the point of being sacrificed; the time of my departure has come. I have fought the good fight, I have finished the race, I have kept the faith. Henceforth there is laid up for me the crown of righteousness, which the Lord will award to me on that Day . . .
>
> The Lord stood by me and gave me strength to proclaim the message fully, that all the Gentiles might hear it. So I was rescued from the lion's mouth. *The Lord will rescue me from every evil and save me for his heavenly kingdom.* To God be the glory for ever and ever. Amen. (2 Tim. 4:6-8, 17-18)

Jesus comforted us with these words, "Even the hairs of your head are all numbered. Fear not." (Lk. 12:7) No matter what happens to us, we can trust in God's providence to bring us safely home. God's protection does not preserve us from dying, but he will bring us through death to new life.

IF TODAY YOU HEAR GOD'S VOICE, HARDEN NOT YOUR HEART

First, the Lord conveyed something comforting to me, "I will protect you." I reveled in that: then came the challenge. The second and final communication that I remember was: "You must justify your soul." It was a pronouncement that I heard and the whole experience conveyed this to me. As I was being filled with love and glory, I also had a major source of discomfort within me. Much like Adam in the garden, I felt naked before God. I was exposed. I was judging myself and I didn't feel right (justified) before God. (This is why I didn't want to go through the tunnel in the first place!) Psalm 90:8 says, "You have set our iniquities before you, our secret sins in the light of your face." My conscience and the state of my soul before God were not right and I knew it. By the way, I believe this was the major reason God brought me before himself. In his mercy, he was showing me the wanting state of my soul and giving me time to change.

People will often say, "How can a loving God send people to hell?" What I discovered through this experience is that God doesn't send anyone to hell; rather, we judge ourselves. All of our secrets, all of our motivations, all of our deeds and all of our thoughts will be laid bare before God. No one can hide from this luminous scrutiny. God's light will penetrate us and we will know how we stand and who we are before God. Paul knew of the coming self-judgment when he wrote, "What the law requires is written on their hearts, while their conscience also bears witness and their conflicting thoughts accuse or perhaps excuse them on that day when, according to my gospel, God judges the secrets of people by Christ Jesus." (Rom. 2:15-16)

The theology of John's Gospel also upholds this type of self-judgment. His gospel has what is called a "realized eschatology." What that means is that the truths having to do with the final days are, in John's view, already being realized. An example of what I mean is the concept of eternal life. Rather than eternal life being something just for the hereafter, it is presented as something for the here and now. In the Gospel of John, it is a new *quality* of life through the Holy Spirit, as well as something that will continue into the future and last forever. In regards to judgment, there will be the judgment on the last day (Jn. 12:48) but there is also the present reality of the judgment. It occurs each day of our lives. *How we live, the choices we make and the deeds we do or don't do now is the judgment.* It is best explained in these words of Jesus, "This is the judgment, that the light has come into the world, and people loved darkness rather than light, because their deeds were evil." (Jn. 3:19) In a very real way, today is your judgment day! When it comes to the judgment, eternity is now. Your choices and your deeds determine your eternal destiny. Either you make faith choices, or choices that disregard God and his will.

The Scriptures teach that after Adam fell he hid from God because he felt naked, ashamed and afraid. (Gen. 3:8) Notice, God had not judged him, Adam judged himself and felt unworthy of the Lord because of what he had done. Then God asked, "Where are you?" (Gen. 3:9) Of course God knew his location, but he was asking Adam a deeper question. What God was asking was, "Where are you before me? What is the state of your soul?" The writer of Genesis is posing that question for all of us to consider. Adam could hide no longer and his disobedience showed his true colors. He was naked in the light of God's awesome presence. He was found out.

This, by the way, is one of the meanings of the often misunderstood term, "the fear of the Lord." It is the fear of being judged. To stand before God knowing you are not right inspires great fear. This holy fear can help motivate us to change our behavior and become right before God. Paul the Apostle stated, "For we must all appear before the judgment seat of Christ, so that each one may receive good or evil, according to what he has done in the body. Therefore, knowing the fear of the Lord, we persuade people." (2 Cor. 5:10-11) This fear of the Lord should not be the motivating factor determining our behavior but it should influence our behavior.

WHO ARE YOU REALLY?

As I stood before God, I experienced a life review. I didn't see all my deeds on a screen, but *who I was as a person* was immediately clear. As I stood there before God's majesty and saw his beauty, love and perfection I knew I was severely lacking. In a flash, my life was laid bare. There was no hiding, no pretending, and no putting on.

At the time, I had just turned 20. I lived the life of most teenagers in college. I drank, smoked, dated and partied with girls. I had no involvement in the community and didn't reach out to anyone in service. My external behavior revealed my interior motivations. My deeds displayed my heart. My life revolved around me. I was all about myself. I was very selfish, narcissistic and stingy. I can remember using people and loving things to make me happy.

I was studying business my first two years in school. My sole goal was to make a lot of money. I wanted to lead a comfortable life. Foremost in my mind was the great American dream of getting a job, accumulating possessions, and living the good life. If I could find a woman who was good-looking enough and met my other criteria, then I might marry. I didn't want to have children. I was too selfish for that. Having children would be too much responsibility and require too much sacrifice.

I had done many things of which I am not proud. I had been dishonest, selfish, lived to party, had many idols, and lived in sexual excess and lust. I had a number of relationships with women that had all ended up with hurt and separation. Much of it was my fault because I was so hard to please. I had shut the God of my childhood out of my life because of my attachment to the world and its pleasures. My heart had become hard and full of doubt.

I distinctly remember sitting in a McDonald's near UMass in Amherst as an 18-year-old freshman when I began to reflect on the way I was living (my conscience was speaking to me). I began to question God interiorly. Instinctively, if you begin to live a reckless life, you rationalize your behavior to yourself. (2 Cor. 10:5) This happens with everyone, I believe, and there are no excuses. I consciously remember thinking to myself, "I may not be living right, but what are the chances there really is a God anyway?"

Little did I know the truth of these two Psalms, "The fool says in his heart, 'There is no God.'" (Ps. 14:1) And "Sin speaks to the wicked deep in his heart; there is no fear of God before his eyes." (Ps. 36:1) In my foolishness, I had been listening to the voice of sin and had grown hard of heart. But God's mercy softens even the hardest of hearts.

Nine months before the time I had this experience with God, I had begun a process of repentance and faith. I was giving myself to Jesus but I still had a long way to go. God revealed to me the depth of my disobedience and the state of my soul.

As I stood before love itself, I realized to my shame that I wasn't even close to being a loving person. The opposite of love is not hate. The opposite of love is selfishness. Love is generous and cares. Selfishness is stingy and cares only for itself. When God mercifully told me that I needed to justify my soul, I understood that the purpose of my life was to journey from self*fish*ness to self*less*ness. Mother Teresa said, "At the end of our life we will not be judged by how many diplomas we have received, how much money we have made, how many great things we have done. We will be judged by 'I was hungry and you gave me to eat. I was naked and you clothed me. I was homeless and you took me in.'" God is a God of hearts. In other words, God is interested in our *true* motivation and our love for others.

I heard a story about one of our Passionist priests. One day as he was driving to do some ministry, his car broke down. When he got out to change the tire, a passing car swerved and accidentally hit him. He flew through the air and hit the ground, stunned but still conscious. In a flash his life passed before him and he heard a voice saying over and over, "How have you loved? How have you loved?" He realized that even though he was a priest and in ministry, he was going through the motions without genuinely loving people. You can be as "religious" as you want to be, but what God is after is love. Jesus taught the religious leaders of his day the same thing. They were complaining because Jesus was eating with tax collectors and sinners. Jesus told them, "Go and learn what this means, 'I desire mercy, and not sacrifice.'" (Mt. 9:13)

A perennial problem in all churches is lack of involvement. Most people go to Mass or services and feel that is enough. They have participated in ritual, given something in the offering and said some prayers. God makes it clear time after time in the Scriptures that ritual is *not* enough. For example, Jesus told the story of the Good Samaritan. (Lk. 10:29-37) A man was stripped and beaten and left for dead by the side of the road. A priest was going up the road and saw him and moved to the other side of the road. A Levite (a born priest) also moved to the other side. (By the way, they were traveling up the hill toward Jerusalem and we can infer they were going there to offer sacrifice.) It was a foreigner, the Samaritan, who stopped to offer aid. Through the medium of a story Jesus is asking, "Who is the truly holy person, the one who offers ritual sacrifice or the one who sacrifices his time and money for a person in need?"

RELIGION = REACHING OUT

True religion is not just about ritual, it is about reaching out.

It is so easy to go to church week after week, hear the Word of God proclaimed, and yet not respond by getting involved. After God touched me when I was 20, I knew that attending Mass was not enough. I had to make some kind of move to help people. "Religion that is pure and undefiled before God the Father is this: to visit orphans and widows in their affliction." (Jas. 1:27) It was clear to me, any way I looked at my faith, that I had to get involved somehow. Religion is all about my *relationship* with God and with people. I knew that I couldn't do everything, but I could do something. I chose to devote myself to helping people in the spiritual realm. I have devoted my passion and energies toward bringing people to salvation and a deep relationship with God. This is what touched me and I want everyone to have it.

As a preacher, I have the responsibility to call people to what lies behind ritual. The Eucharist may be the "font and summit" of our faith as the documents declare, but it is really meant to be a catalyst for more. Mass is a beginning, not an end in itself. At the conclusion of Mass we proclaim the great commission, "*Go* in love and peace, to serve the Lord and each other." Strengthened by the prayer and the body and blood of Christ, we are to *go*, not stay put and close in on ourselves.

One Sunday I was worshipping the Lord at Mass with some lay partners involved in my ministry. The Gospel reading that Sunday was the story of the rich man and a poor beggar named Lazarus. (Lk. 16:19-31) The rich man had ample opportunity to help Lazarus "at his gate" but he never did. Both died and there was a great reversal. Suddenly the first became last and the last, first. Lazarus enjoyed heaven while the rich man cried out in lament and regret. I let the truth of God's Word really speak to me and penetrate me. I tried not to deny what I was hearing or just "get through Mass" and go on with my life. I let the Gospel challenge me and convict me. During Mass, as part of the homily, my friends and I talked about an action step that we could take as a ministry team.

My part of the action step had to do with my ministry as a priest and preacher. I sensed God calling me to invite each person who comes to my missions to make a move toward helping other people. I now do this on the final night of my mission as I proclaim the Holy Spirit. Before the final night I communicate with the social justice committee and the evangelization people to try to find out what the needs of the local community are. During my talk I try to inspire the people to reach out to the needy "at their gates." There are many ways to get involved by joining a liturgical or teaching ministry at church, a social justice ministry that reaches out to the poor and hungry, or an evangelization ministry that spreads the Gospel in the local community.

I call this program of involvement "You *can* make a difference." At the conclusion of the mission, I usually have a sheet or many sheets of paper at a table staffed by the various committee members. The sheets of paper are entitled "I want to make a difference." There is a place to sign your name and give your address and phone number. A member of that particular committee will call you and help you become involved with the outreach of your choice. I have been doing this now for over a year and it has been very successful. I find that many people are looking for a way to get involved and just don't know how. I am especially impressed with how many elderly people are signing up. Of course not everyone signs up to get involved, but many do. The Holy Spirit always leads people to deeper meaning and to reaching out to those hurting in the community.

In addition I sensed the Lord wanted me to sow seed back into each community I visit. Everywhere I preach I bring my books, tapes and videos. I sell these teachings and at some missions the royalties can be quite substantial. God was inviting me, through his Word that Sunday, to give back 10% of my royalties on all my teachings to the particular community where I am ministering. (The other 90% goes into my ministry fund to enable me to buy equipment, print books and reach out in various other ways.) This tithe is done as a seed so that the particular program where the money is needed will benefit. I believe that the seeds sown help the sales of my books to prosper well in other cities. You will be glad to know that if you bought this book at a mission, 10% of your money went back into social justice programs in your own community.

Reaching out is true religion. Jesus taught often about being rich in God's eyes, to "lay up for yourselves treasure in heaven." (Mt. 6:19-21) I believe that he was talking about our personal relationship with God as well as reaching out to other people with our time, talents and finances. That is what truly makes us rich! St. Lawrence, a deacon and martyr who lived in the third century, was ordered by his Roman captors to "bring out the treasure of the church and place it before them." St. Lawrence gathered all the poor and the lame, brought them out and said, "These people are the true treasures of the Church." Those words would get him martyred.

There is no such thing as "private religion." If you want to follow Christ, just like him you must deny yourself and take up your cross of obedience daily. Reaching out to others can be a sacrifice at times, but it is very rewarding. I fly high each time I finish a mission. There is nothing like getting a letter from someone telling me how much I helped them. Helping people is the meaning of life and the hallmark of love. Actually, something ironic happens when

I am reaching out. I begin to take my mind off of myself and my problems and end up being radically blessed!

I heard a story that illustrates this well. Two monks from opposite sides of the globe were walking and talking about their various beliefs. As they were walking up the hill toward the monastery, it began to snow. An hour later they heard the moans of a man who had fallen down a ravine and was almost unconscious. The first monk said, "We must stop to help him." The other monk said, "The storm is getting worse, we'll never make it back if we stop now." The first monk replied, "The heart of my religion is mercy. I must stop and help." As he carefully sidestepped his way down the 50-foot ravine, the other monk proceeded on.

When the monk got to the man, he was alive but coming in and out of consciousness. The monk lifted the man around his shoulders and slowly carried him on his back. The road was steep and it was a hard climb. He began to sweat even though there was a cold snowstorm. After about an hour, he neared the safe haven of the monastery. Suddenly, he almost tripped as he bumped into what he thought was a tree stump in the snow. As he looked down, he realized that it wasn't a tree stump, it was the other monk. The blizzard-like conditions had overtaken him and he fell and froze to death. Because the first monk had carried the wounded person, he had worked up a sweat and the heat of his exertion kept his own body warm enough so that the cold did not overwhelm him.

His burden became his blessing!

That's the way love and reaching out to others is. When I focus on myself and close my heart to compassion,

I freeze. I have little meaning in my life and am all caught up in myself and my problems. It's easy to get caught up in the petty little things of life and grow in despair. However, when I make the decision to reach out to others and help them, it may be difficult but it keeps me alive. The demanding challenge of the Gospel actually gives me life. Any difficulties or hardships that I bear turn into meaning and joy for me. Helping others is what Christianity is all about.

CHOOSE TO LOVE

Love is a multifaceted gem. First of all, psychologists tell us that love is a decision. They are right. In the realm of the will, it is the choice to reach out to another, to help another and to forgive. Love must not be an isolated choice once in a while. It must be a series of right choices over and over again. It must override what you sometimes feel. For example, I don't always feel like getting on a plane, flying thousands of miles and sleeping in a musty, dusty spare room in order to preach and counsel all day. But I choose to do it over and over again, no matter how I feel. If we just lived in the realm of how we felt, nothing would ever get done. Consistent choices can overcome feelings. These right choices become an attitude and attitudes lead a person to become a person of love. Love is a summation of quality decisions that steers the path of your life.

Love is also affection. It is heartfelt care. You must grow to be a person who cares. True care will move you to reach out. In the story of the Good Samaritan, it was the Samaritan's *compassion* that moved him to help. Jesus taught and fed people because he was moved with compassion. (Mk. 6:34)

Lawrence Kohlberg was a professor at Harvard University. He started as a developmental psychologist and moved into the area of moral education. He posited a theory of moral development. According to his theory, people progress in their moral reasoning through a series of stages. There are six identifiable stages divided into three distinct levels. Kohlberg believed that in order for you to progress, you had to go through each successive stage and could not jump stages. He worked with the question: "What motivates people ethically?"

First, there is the obedience and punishment stage. That is when you behave a certain way because an authority figure has told you to. Secondly, there is the view that you will act morally according to your own best interests. Next, you act to gain the approval of others. The fourth stage has to do with following law and doing things out of obligation and duty. Fifth, you behave a certain way out of genuine interest in the welfare of others. Finally, and very few ever reach this stage, you completely follow the dictates of your conscience instead of black-and-white law.

I believe that mature followers of Jesus are those who genuinely like and care for others and follow a well-formed conscience. They do the right thing even when the wrong thing is happening to them. They do the right thing because it is right even though there seems to be no immediate reward or pleasure. They do the right thing even when no one is watching. Integrity is forged behind closed doors as well as in the open.

St. Paul the Apostle wrote a stirring letter to the churches of Galatia. His letter had to do with freedom from the laws of Moses and liberty in Christ. He talked a lot about how Jesus had come to make us right with God through faith. "For freedom Christ has set us free." (Gal. 5:1) The law, rules and regulations no longer bind us. Our faith in Jesus justifies us. Included in chapter 5 of this liberating letter is a little known but crucial verse, "For in Christ Jesus neither circumcision or uncircumcision is of any avail, but faith *made effective* through love." (Gal. 5:6)

In other words, Paul was saying that the heart of Christianity is not obedience to a set of laws; rather, it is faith in the person of Jesus. Our faith is not an intellectual assent to a doctrine, but belief in and commitment to a person, Jesus. What makes our faith live is love. Love is the wind that drives the sails of faith. Love activates faith. Faith alone is dead. We must do the good works which are the fruit of our faith. God is love and we must become love.

When I stood before love itself in my vision, I knew that I was mostly selfish and had little love to show for my life. Yes, I loved my parents and myself, but I had hardly reached out to anyone outside my nuclear family. Because of my lack of love-development, I learned that I could not be filled with God's love and glory as fully as I wanted to be. I stood there penetrated by the glory of God, yet I felt there was in me an inability to receive fully and enjoy more intensely because of the state of my soul. This caused me anguish and distress. I know it was the Lord teaching me in that moment that I must grow. I know that the purpose of my life and one of the reasons I was sent back to this earth is to mature into a person of love. The purpose of our life on earth is to journey from selfishness to selflessness. This sanctification and growth occurs through the purification process. The meaning of human existence is love. As we grow in love now, our capacity to receive God now and later will expand.

OUR CALL TO LOVE

Jesus taught about love all the time. "By this will all know that you are my disciples, if you have love one for another." (Jn. 13:35) The centerpiece of Jesus' important Sermon on the Mount was, "You, therefore, must be perfect, as your heavenly Father is perfect." (Mt. 5:48) Many incorrectly interpret Jesus' words as setting an impossible standard of utter and complete perfection. Rather, the word perfection in the Greek has to do with a goal and achieving maturity, becoming complete. This comment followed Jesus' teaching about loving even enemies. Therefore what Jesus was really teaching here was that the goal or purpose of our life is to mature in love and have love as our goal. We must strive to be God-like.

The fathers of the Second Vatican Council promulgated a document on the renewal of religious life that called all communities back to the roots of their original charisms. This document was called *Perfectae Caritatis* (The Perfection of Love). More than anything else, the call to religious life is a vocation to love. In this document we are told, "The pursuit of perfect charity by the means of the evangelical counsels (vows) traces its origin to Jesus himself." It is "under the impulse of love which the Holy Spirit pours into their hearts that religious live for Christ and for his Body, the Church."

Similarly, two people enter into the sacrament of matrimony to become one person. It is this "becoming" that God is interested in. Selfishness melts into the selflessness of giving one's body to the other even when you don't feel like it. You become one when you apologize for hurting the other and admit you are wrong. You grow in love when you give even when you feel your spouse isn't reciprocating. You mature when you forgive seventy times seven. You come to perfection in the trials and difficulties and joys of creating and raising children. Submitting to each other is never easy, but makes each person grow.

Single life too, is a vocation and a call to love. Certainly being there for your family is important, but you must extend yourself beyond your nuclear family. You do this by getting involved in the community. Reaching out to those who have less and making a difference in their lives is important. Spreading the Gospel by the way you live and speak is your call. Achieving excellence and moral integrity by your choices in life is your vocation.

Whatever your vocation is in life, your call is to *love*. I know from experience that I have been given more time in my life because I am called to be generous, caring and forgiving. As we submit and surrender to God through the circumstances in which we find ourselves, he will ripen the wonderful fruit of love in us. The extent to which we live with passion, learn, and grow in love now will determine our capacity to receive love when we stand before the majesty of love itself.

7
WORK OUT YOUR OWN SALVATION

The first words I heard from God was a comforting "I will protect you." The second and final words I remember in his presence was challenging. God told me, "You must justify your soul." The dictionary defines justify as: "to show to be just, right, or in accord with reason, to warrant." In the Old Testament a just person referred to one who was acquitted or vindicated before a judge's tribunal. That happened before God by keeping the Mosaic Law. Keeping the law perfectly was and is a tremendously difficult task. I've heard it said once that justification is "just-as-if" you have never sinned. Of course we are all sinners, so how can we be justified?

We are told in the New Testament, Jesus is our justification. (1 Cor. 6:11) Galatians 2:16 tells us clearly that we are not justified by our own works but by faith in Jesus. Whenever I meditate on the Stations of the Cross, the first station strikes me: Jesus is condemned. I believe with all my heart that when he stood before Pilate, he was taking my place. I should have been condemned because of all my sins. But, mysteriously, God accepted Jesus' willing sacrifice on my behalf. Because Jesus was condemned, "there is therefore now no condemnation for those who are in Christ Jesus." (Rom. 8:1) Jesus' condemnation, suffering, death, and resurrection were all for me. When I was baptized into him, I was baptized into his death so that I could rise to a new life of justification.

There are *two* components of justification. One has to do with the state of being forgiven for all your sins. Because of the grace of forgiveness, you can stand before the Holy One. The other dimension that many forget about has to do with the process of *being made* righteous or just. In justification we are declared right before God *and made* upright. In Jesus we have been vindicated and declared innocent and forgiven by his blood. In addition, in Jesus we "*become* the very righteousness of God." (2 Cor. 5:21)

What does it mean to *become* the righteousness of God? Essentially there must be grace and our cooperation. God has freely communicated to us the virtue of Christ his son. This infusion of the justice of Jesus is a major part of justification. All that Jesus is, lives within us. This free gift is in all of us in seed form because Jesus is present. The fruit of the Spirit is in us and needs to ripen. (Gal. 5:22-23) God's righteousness is his forgiving, generous, merciful, compassionate, just and loving character. The goal of our lives is to allow this character of God to emerge from us. (It must be worked out of us.)

When I stood before God, he told me that I must justify my soul. Through his grace, I was forgiven and declared upright before him by the blood of Jesus. Legally, I am innocent and upright. It all happened through the blood of the Cross. However, experientially, because I was so selfish and non-virtuous, God was telling me that I needed to change.

A major part of justification has to do with a continuous act of will. It means that my thoughts become Christ-like and that my emotions are managed. Now I must allow Jesus to become all that I am. My heart must be reshaped. I must be molded and transformed. I have become a new creation. The seeds of this beautiful new life are within me. Every day I am in the process of making the decision to let them blossom fully.

Make no mistake about it. There is a responsibility *on our part* in the area of justification. Some would say that we are totally justified, once and for all, by Christ. We are already justified in that we are forgiven, but we need to become Christ-like and in order for that to happen, our effort is required. Our responsibility is to participate in and cooperate with the grace of God. In practical terms, this means agreeing with and surrendering to the Spirit of Jesus in us every day. As we change and grow, we are not earning heaven in any way; rather, we are becoming a new person in Christ.

HAVE THIS MIND AMONG YOU . . . (PHIL. 2:5)

In the process of justification, you allow Jesus to "work out of" yourself so he becomes all that you are. You begin to think like him (we have the mind of Christ – 1 Cor. 2:16), behave like him and surrender your will to God as he did. "He was the first born of many brothers and sisters," we are told in Romans 8:29. That extremely crucial verse in the New Testament tells us that we were actually predestined to be conformed to the image of Jesus. Justification and our life in Christ is the process of being conformed and transformed. Becoming justified doesn't mean that we are another Christ, but we are Christ-ians, partisans of Christ and his disciples. There is only one master and messiah. Now, through God's free gift, we are mystically grafted on the vine and become one with him. He is the vine and we the branches.

Justification is a process. Being transformed takes time. So in a very real sense we can say that we *are* justified (forgiven, acquitted and possessing Christ within) and we also *are being* justified (becoming virtuous and holy).

One of the sticking points of the Protestant reformation was this doctrine of justification. Martin Luther sensed that people were trying to get right with God through their own deeds, prayers and good works. People were purchasing indulgences and seemingly "buying" their way into heaven. This irked him greatly and flew in the face of what he knew to be true from the Scriptures. The Bible clearly teaches that no one is good enough and that all of us have sinned. If we break one command, we have broken them all. Therefore, no matter how hard we try we can never earn or buy our way into heaven. We need a savior. One of the major reasons for the split in Christendom was Luther's teaching that we are saved by grace through faith in Jesus. In Luther's opinion, Catholics were teaching that we are saved by works as well as grace.

As recently as the year 2000, as I wrote in my first book *Live Passionately!*, Catholics and Lutherans finally reached an agreement about how to be right with God. The *Joint Declaration on Justification by Faith* states the new position. "Together we confess: by grace alone, in faith in Christ's saving work and not because of any merit on our part, we are accepted by God and receive the Holy Spirit, who renews our hearts while equipping and calling us to good works." In other words, it is not by faith and good works that we are saved. It is rather our faith in the saving action of Jesus that justifies us, shapes our character, *and* spurs us on to do good works. God does the renewing with our constant cooperation.

I think when push comes to shove this modern day declaration states what the Catholic Church has always believed. The reformation has helped us to define this more clearly. The *Catechism of the Catholic Church* proclaims, "Our justification comes from the grace of God. Grace is favor, the free and undeserved help that God gives us to respond to his call to become children of God, adoptive sons and daughters, partakers of the divine nature and of eternal life." (#1996) Justification, therefore, has to do with being put right before God through God's initiative. We are justified when we are forgiven and made righteous. Since we lost our initial innocence through sin and none is righteous, we need a savior. It is our faith in Jesus and his transforming presence within us that secures for us a place in the divine presence.

The only reason I had these experiences with God is because I was justified through the free gift of Jesus at the Cross!

I want to reaffirm that not only does Jesus take our place at Calvary; justification has to do with the process of Jesus *taking our place in our hearts*. In this way it is closely related to sanctification. Sanctification is the process of being purified and made holy. When we come to Christ by faith, he literally gives us a new heart. The process of rebirth, regeneration and transformation occurs. Ezekiel the prophet had prophesied that God would "give them a new heart, and put a new spirit within them; I will take the stony heart out of their flesh and give them a heart of flesh they may walk in my statutes and keep my ordinances and obey them." (Ez. 11:19) Paul the Apostle put it this way, "I have been crucified with Christ; it is no longer I who live, but Christ who lives in me; and the life I now live in the flesh I live by faith in the Son of God, who loved me and gave himself for me." (Gal. 2:20) The miracle of justification is becoming one with Christ who lives in us. It is allowing Jesus to influence our thoughts, decisions, emotions and actions.

Justification, then, is all about being right with God. It occurs primarily through the free gift of God. We cannot earn this. Nothing we can do merits eternal life. As we come to Jesus in faith and accept, receive and believe in his Cross-death for us, we are redeemed from sin and made right with God. We are now justified in his presence. Through the blood of Jesus we are declared right and are just-as-if we have never sinned. This is wonderful Good News. The blood of a spotless lamb (Jesus) is central. In the Old Testament the countless blood sacrifices of animals foreshadowed the blood sacrifice of Jesus. We are told in the book of Hebrews, "Without the shedding of blood, there is no forgiveness of sins." (9:22)

However, being innocent and forgiven isn't enough. We must show that we belong in God's holy presence. We must be just-ified (infused with justice). God's call for us is to show forth virtue and "be holy as God is holy." (1 Pet. 1:16) Justification is the lifelong process of becoming Christ-like. We *already* have the righteousness of God in us through the free gift of his Son in us. We must allow Christ-in-us to become Christ-through-us and out-of-us. In other words, what is in us must be worked out through us and become all that we are.

We can be sure that our sins are forgiven now. We can also be certain that God is calling each of us to become the fullness of a new creature in his Son. We must cooperate with the grace of God in us. Cooperating with grace means that we avoid sin by the strength of the Holy Spirit. Additionally, our life must be about allowing love and the character of Christ to work out of us. We must grow in virtue and maturity. We choose to develop an excellent character. We choose to become a loving person. We allow the mind of Christ to possess our mind. We are called to achieve our potential. God's will is that we become the image of Jesus of Nazareth. This is what it means to be justified.

When God said, "You must be justified," I knew I needed to change. I was convicted and convinced. I was also being given another chance. God was graciously giving me more time. He was telling me my life's purpose. At the time I didn't understand that it would be a lifelong process. Now, years later, I have deeper understanding and a goal set before me. This goal ought to be the striving of *every* person on earth. "God has predestined us to be *conformed to the image of his son* in order that he might be the firstborn of many brothers and sisters." (Rom. 8:29)

DIVINE APPOINTMENT

I have been preaching evangelistic missions all over the United States and Canada since 1990. It is important to try to find a "catchy" title or theme that will grab the people. Although I have changed my talks many times, I have stayed with one consistent theme: "Come *Encounter* Jesus." I want my preaching, my writing, and my tapes and videos to be places where people encounter Jesus. In the dictionary the word encounter means "a meeting with another, sometimes unexpected." Synonyms are "a coming together, contact, an appointment or rendezvous."

I believe with all my heart that God wants us to encounter him. This has been validated time and time again by my experiences. It may not always be a dramatic meeting, but God wants us to know him nevertheless. The epiphany (manifestation of God) can occur anywhere. For example, the apostle Paul was traveling, Peter was working and Isaiah was worshipping. Yet all three encountered God in the midst of their daily activities.

There are a multitude of examples of God revealing himself to people in the Bible. Moses met God at the burning bush. Isaiah had a vision of God in the temple. Paul met the Lord on the road to Damascus. The Virgin Mary had a visitation from an angel in her home. In all these stories there are common elements. First there is an encounter with God. Next there is fear. Lastly there is a call of some sort. One story that illustrates these elements involves the apostle Peter. This story has been called the story of the "unexpected catch" and it comes from Luke 5:1-11.

In the story, Peter, a professional fisherman, has worked hard all night and caught nothing. Jesus asked to get into his boat in order to use it for preaching purposes. What was it that he taught that day? Perhaps it was about how our lives can be incredibly fruitful if we follow him. Maybe he taught that if we live by grit we will be frustrated, but if we live by grace, we can experience abundance. Could be that he taught how he came to free us from the law and bring our hearts to rebirth. Whatever it was that he taught the people, he was about to demonstrate something to Peter. He invited Peter to put out into the deep for a catch.

Before this story, we haven't met Peter in the Gospel of Luke. We can infer that Peter knew something about Jesus because he let him use his boat. Another indication is that Peter answered Jesus' request with "Master." In Luke, this is a remark of respect because the word used is the Greek translation of rabbi or teacher. Apparently Peter already had been impressed with this Galilean preacher.

THE FEAR OF THE LORD

When the boat launched out into the deep, although the apostles knew how to fish and had fished all night and caught nothing, they caught so many fish that their nets began to break and their boats began to sink. Suddenly Peter came face-to-face with the divine side of Jesus for the first time. It was an eye-opening encounter that led to an interesting response. We are told that "When Peter saw the catch, he fell down at Jesus' knees, saying, 'Depart from me, for I am a sinful man, O Lord.'" (Lk. 5:8)

First of all, there was the recognition of Jesus as *Lord*. Notice the progression. He began by calling him a teacher, but now he realized exactly who was aboard his boat. Then came the classic response that a person has when they meet God: he was afraid. We know this because he felt sinful, knelt down and asked Jesus to go away from him. At this Jesus told Peter, "Don't be afraid."

This fear is the fear of the Lord. When Moses encountered God at the burning bush, "he hid his face, for he was *afraid* to look at God." (Ex. 3:6) When Isaiah met God in the temple, he cried, "Woe is me! For I am lost; for I am a man of unclean lips and I dwell in the midst of a people of unclean lips; for with my own eyes I have seen the King, the Lord of hosts!" (Is. 6:6) During the transfiguration, Peter, James and John fell on their faces and they were exceedingly afraid. (Mt. 17:6) Even Mary was so troubled that the angel said, "Don't be afraid Mary." (Lk. 1:30)

All of these biblical characters experienced a sense of their own unworthiness and felt fear. This fear came as they became aware of the imminent presence of God. The fear was a sense of awe and reverence. Peter knew that Jesus was more than just an ordinary human being. He wasn't quite sure what to do.

The fear of the Lord is one of the seven gifts of the Holy Spirit listed by the prophet Isaiah in 11:2-3. Isaiah was telling us that when the Messiah comes, he will have these gifts. It is inspiring to think that Jesus' "delight" was the fear of the Lord. In other words, he walked in God's holy presence. He revered God and never sinned. He knew that God was always present and watching and willed never to offend God in any way. These seven gifts of the Holy Spirit are given to any believer and are celebrated at the sacrament of confirmation. When a person becomes a mature Christian, he or she ought to be walking in the fear of the Lord, with a sense of God's presence, always. Because of the fear of the Lord a person will guard their heart, mind, mouth and actions.

The wisdom literature of the Bible (Proverbs, Sirach, Wisdom) has a lot to say about the fear of the Lord.

> The fear of the Lord is glory and exultation, and gladness and a crown of rejoicing. The fear of the Lord delights the heart, and gives gladness and joy and long life. With the one who fears the Lord it will go well at the end; on the day of his death he will be blessed. To fear the Lord is the beginning of wisdom.
>
> (Sir. 1:11-14)

Many might think that I am advocating going back to the 1950's when preachers tried to scare people into holiness. Some preached that God was out to watch people's every move and if they made any false step, they were bound for hell. There was an image of a harsh, angry, vindictive God proclaimed and believed in back then. I am not saying that at all! The fear of the Lord is not about harshness and punishment, but about reverence. It has to do with appreciating how close our God is to us. It is about realizing his presence and not wanting to offend his love. Yes, to some degree, it is about fear of being judged, but that is not the primary message.

As I wrote before, I think we live in an age when it is popular for people to make God out to be anything they want him to be. Often God is a "buddy" and most anything goes because God is love. For example, some say it is okay to live together out of wedlock because God understands. Others think that an active homosexual lifestyle is permissible because God is forgiving. Still others reason they can abuse their body with food or alcohol and God will overlook this.

I think what is needed today is balanced, solid teaching about the holiness and majesty of God. Yes, God is loving and very compassionate and forgiving. However we cannot just presume God's mercy because of some culture-shaped idea of God that we have floating around in our heads. We need to ground ourselves in the true biblical notion of just who God is. God is mercy, but he is also justice. There needs to be balance and reverence for God. I think the pendulum swung too far to the side of punishment back in the 50's. In much the same way, it has swung too far to the side of "God will forgive anything" in the new millennium.

The fear of the Lord has a lot to do with faith and believing that God is always near. If we know that God is near and notices every thought, motivation and deed, we will want to live uprightly and be pleasing to God. When I was in God's presence I was given the gift of the fear of the Lord. It is a gift that doesn't go away. It is the sense that God is present in every activity and scrutinizes the person that we are. The fear of the Lord is also the truth that one day we will have to stand before God and account for the person we become.

THE PRECIOUS NAME OF JESUS

I find it interesting that when Isaiah had his spectacular vision of God, he became tormented by his sinful words. After I had my vision of God, one of the first areas God called me to change was my speech. I had a terrible swearing habit and took God's name in vain quite often. Habitually, without thinking, I would simply say, "Jesus." I wasn't calling upon him in prayer; I was just saying his name carelessly. I didn't even realize that I was doing it! As God began to deal with me about my mouth, I became aware of how I was using his name wrongly. Jesus said, "By your words you will be justified and by your words you will be condemned." (Mt. 12:37) Words are indicators of where your heart is. Are you right with God? Are you justified? Pay attention to your mouth and you will know where you stand.

You can tell that you fear the Lord when you think before you speak. You don't just spout off at the mouth when something happens. Because you know God is there you are careful. Often when I am golfing and people know that I am a priest, they will be extra careful about saying something offensive. Even some of the worst-behaved people clean up their act very quickly. I can see them struggling to hold their temper and words. They are trying because they know I am there. In the same way, we can control ourselves because we know God is there.

I overcame swearing through God's grace and cooperation. This is part of my justification process. First

I became aware that I had a swearing problem. Then I admitted to myself that I had a problem. I had the will to stop. I asked God to help me. Then every time I was in a situation where I was about to swear, I noticed that I would think the word before I spoke it. This happened in a flash. Whenever I would begin to think a swear word, I stopped and asked God to help me. Every once in a while I would slip and swear. I tried not to let it get me down too much. I kept pressing on and trying. Before long, my mouth was purified and I have much victory in this area now. In the Old Testament, an angel's blazing tong touched the tongue of Isaiah and he was cleansed. This signified the forgiving and cleansing power of grace. We need grace to have victory in this area. We need to cooperate with God's grace, too, by taking responsibility for our words.

I heard a story about a pastor who was riding his sleek new bicycle down the street. As he rode he saw one of his altar servers, Johnny, standing on a lawn trying to start a lawnmower. The pastor stopped and asked, "Johnny, what are you doing?" As he pulled the cord furiously, he replied, "I'm trying to get this thing started . . . so I can earn enough money . . . to buy a bike . . . (looking at the pastor's bike) just like yours!" The pastor thought to himself for a minute and said, "Hey, I need a lawnmower and you need a bike. Why don't we just switch?" Johnny smiled and said, "Deal!"

Next thing you know the pastor is bent over the lawnmower pulling the cord. He straightened up and said, "Johnny, how do you get this thing started?" "You gotta swear at it!" "What?" replied the pastor, "I'm a priest. I don't swear. I don't even remember how to swear!" To this Johnny replied, "You keep pulling on that cord and it'll come back to you!"

When you pray for the gift of the fear of the Lord, you are praying to encounter God's presence so you will live in holy awe and reverence. You will have a sense of God wherever you go and you will not want to offend God. You will have the grace to want to please God all the time. You will think before you act and even before you talk. God's marvelous presence is with us always. Love God so much that you "delight in the fear of the Lord."

GOD PLEASER OR PEOPLE PLEASER?

In addition, when you have the gift of the fear of the Lord, you will begin to prize what God thinks of you more than you care what people think. We have all grown up with a sense of wanting to be people pleasers and we worry about acceptance and agonize over "what people think." When God touches a person with his magnificent presence a new freedom occurs. The classic example was Peter. He denied Jesus on the night he was betrayed. He was afraid of the Jews and lived behind locked doors. Then the glorious, powerful presence of God overwhelmed him at Pentecost. Suddenly he went from a marshmallow to a bold proclaimer of Jesus. People were struck at the boldness of the apostles in the face of danger. Peter and the others were thrown into prison and then brought before the Jewish council of religious leaders and warned not to speak in Jesus' name. They replied, "We must obey God rather than men." (Acts 5:29)

I have struggled with self-image and feelings of inadequacy all of my life. Because of that I have had panic attacks and a lot of anxiety. Without help from God, there is no way I ever could have gotten up in front of the people and preached. It is fearing God more than people that has helped me become a bold, authoritative preacher. John tells us that perfect love casts out all fear. (1 Jn. 4:18) One facet of loving God is fearing him. I am still being perfected in this area. This fear of God has helped me to overcome the fears I have of public speaking. I still feel fear, but I manage it through God's help.

Presently, God is dealing with me about preaching new, untried material. Rather than always preaching my "safe" sermons, God keeps leading me forward to proclaim new, bold truth. I am striving to be ever more challenging and to care less about popularity and more about God. Although I still feel insecure about myself deep within, I value what God wants more than I value my ego. I lift up my uncomfortable feelings to God as they happen, then I find great blessing and help from God to go through and manage them. Don't run from unpleasant feelings. The only way to come to healing is to face them and go through.

YOU ARE CALLED AND CHOSEN (1 PET. 2:9)

Immediately after Peter and other biblical characters encountered the divine presence, they experienced a call. For example, God asks Isaiah, "*Whom* shall I send and *who* will go for us?" (Is. 6:8) In Peter's case, Jesus said, "Do not be afraid. From now on you will be a fisher of men and women." (Lk. 5:10) Whether you have had a dramatic "visitation" from God or not, *you* are called, too.

Something happened as I was writing this book that really touched my heart. I have been a member of a vocation team along with seven lay people for years. I have preached on the road for twelve years at the time of this writing. I have prayed for vocations to the priesthood with others and have preached about it all over the U.S. While I truly believe I am sowing seeds in the hearts of many young people, I have only had a few nibbles. Despite all my efforts, no one had joined the Passionists.

Last Advent, however, I was preaching at St. Louis Church in Austin, Texas. The final night I was proclaiming the Holy Spirit and the Lord led me to talk about vocations to the priesthood. Unbeknownst to me, there was a 27-year-old young man with his girlfriend in the congregation. He had some background in lay ministry, and was also dating. I proclaimed that God is still calling people to the priesthood. When I did, his girlfriend nudged him with her elbow and smiled. He said that at that moment, he wanted to make a move toward God but wasn't sure what to do. Eventually he would know!

To make a long story short, months later he moved to Houston and was directed to visit our Passionist community by a diocesan priest. Little did he know when he showed up at our door that he would meet me! When we eventually talked he said that he had felt a call to priesthood from his boyhood, yet he never acted on it. The mission was a catalyst to help him to discuss it and make a move. He is now in the process of discernment. Should he make this committment, he will be an outstanding priest and religious. In addition to this young man, I know of others who are discerning a call to the priesthood and sisterhood.

What we must understand about a call is that we have it from our mother's womb. (Jer. 1:5) God implants it within us even before we are born. As we journey through various stages of the life cycle, we can become more or less susceptible to "receiving" this call. You receive a call when you come to God in prayer and experience his blessing. Once people get in touch with and identify God's call, they will discover that it was there all their life, only they may not have known it. No one "gets" God's call at a certain point in his or her life. Rather, they *discover* what was already there all along.

I speak from experience. When God touched me in these near death experiences, I didn't automatically presume that I had a vocation to the priesthood. I knew I had a call to be a Christian, but the rest unfolded in subsequent years. After years of discernment, questioning, confusion, doubt and prayer, I finally understood that I didn't "get" a call when I turned to God at age 19, I *discovered* what was already in God's mind from all eternity! I am so glad that I searched and looked. Perhaps there is nothing so tragic as to come to the end of your life having missed God's plan and call for your life.

GIVE YOUR ALL TO YOUR CALL

I believe there are many young men and women out there who have awesome calls from God to become priests, brothers, and sisters and they haven't dug deep enough to find those calls. Many of our young people are so gifted and talented. Others have untapped potential. I sincerely believe that in order for a young person to want to become a religious they have to first of all *have an encounter with God*. Without an encounter, a touch, why would anyone want to be a religious? The life is too demanding and challenging and radical to seek it in and of itself. I really believe that if our young people will sincerely and authentically seek Jesus they will have experiences of his mercy. Many would be filled with the Holy Spirit and power. Still others would know the joy of rebirth. This touch of God is what they need in order for them to discover their call as a priest or sister.

One of my roles as a preacher is to simply proclaim Jesus and a personal relationship with him. As people find this "pearl of great price" then some will discover another treasure within, a call to the priesthood or sisterhood and religious life. In addition to this basic call to relationship with Jesus, I also encourage those who already know Jesus to look within and discover his will for their lives. Some have a call to the priesthood; others have a call toward married life and raising children. The Church also recognizes the gift of a call to the single life. Being single for the Lord is a valid, powerful call. What is important is living for Jesus, no matter what vocation calls you.

The simple truth is that God has a plan for our life! This plan is for welfare and a future and a hope. (Jer. 29:11) As we honestly search out this plan, we *can* discover it. Having gone through years discerning my call to the priesthood, let me tell you that it is not easy grasping it. Searching for God's call takes a lot of self-honesty and faith. It also takes trusting, risking, and launching out into the deep. Nothing is written in stone or black and white, but God does write his will within our hearts and consciences. His will must be prayed about and discerned.

I'LL GET BY WITH A LITTLE HELP
FROM MY FRIENDS

If you are a person who thinks you may have a call from God to become a religious (priest, brother or sister), you need the help of a spiritual director. A director can be a man or a woman, a priest or a layperson. You should choose a mature person of faith you can trust and talk to easily. It is too hard to sort out a call on your own. You need the help of the community to discern. Talking with someone else will help you hear what is within you. It will help you to clear up the confusion and the conflicting feelings. You also need objective views. A spiritual director may give you ideas you have never considered. You must get in touch with your heart. What is within you? What are your desires? Be assured that God wants you to be happy. He does not call you to a life of misery.

Along with praying and talking it out with someone, you must give yourself time. If you have an authentic call to become a religious, this call will not fade. The desire within may not always be burning and be at the forefront of your thoughts, but it will consistently appear. Time will tell whether you are called or not. God's call is irrevocable and will endure. If the desire to serve as a religious remains in you over time, most likely you do have a call. Jeremiah said, "If I say I will not mention God or speak any more in his name, there is in my heart as it were a burning fire shut up in my bones, I am weary with holding it in and I cannot." (Jer. 20:9) When a person applies to our community we always make them wait for a season. Time tells us if the call remains as vibrant as when they apply.

Even when you feel you have discovered a certain call, it still takes faith to believe that it actually is a personal call for you from God. Although I am years into living my call as a Passionist, there are many times when I feel duped and think to myself, "Am I really called or did I just imagine all this?" I'm sure many married people feel the same way at times. I especially feel like this when I disagree with those I live with or when I don't preach very well. But I know that I must walk by faith and not by sight. The validity of our call is shown not just by how we feel or how we perform. In a major decision such as a life call, God does not dupe us or let us miss the mark.

Sometimes a married man will seek my counsel, questioning whether or not he should have become a priest. "Did I make a mistake?" he asks. I don't think so. People follow their heart the best they can at the particular time when they are making life choices. I really believe that God will work through any choice we make. God wants us to be happy and live for him. If you are married, try not to regret your choice. Live your marriage wholeheartedly. If you are a religious, live passionately for Jesus. God is pleased with whatever vocation you have discerned as long as you stay committed and live faithfully.

Any authentic vocation from God is a call to selflessness. Discipleship is all about denying yourself, taking up your cross daily and following Jesus. In religious life there are many times when I have to let go of my own wants and ideas and acquiesce to the group. Religious life is also a call to service. According to our talents, we put ourselves at the service of the community. In order to minister well, I must say "Yes" to God over and over again.

For example, writing books takes discipline. I have had to give up many golf games and T.V. programs in order to do this. There have been many sunny days when I would rather have been outside enjoying a rest. I have worked on my books during vacations, on airplanes, and in rectory bedrooms on the road. Writing takes effort and creativity. There are endless delays. I have to coordinate with lay partners and printers to get each book project finished in its entirety. Whenever I finish working each day I have such a sense of satisfaction. I know that I am accomplishing God's will for my life and sowing seeds of blessing into others' lives. When the book is finished and printed I look at the finished product like a proud father. Saying "Yes" to God means giving yourself to your particular vocation.

Marriage is a call to say "Yes" to God by honoring your spouse. Selflessness is shown when you let an argument drop or forgive for the thousandth time. It means cleaning the house or going to work with a good attitude. Having children and the demands they impose on a relationship requires self-surrender also. Similarly, single people deny themselves when they serve as a C.C.D. teacher. Instead of going out drinking and partying, others selflessly remain home and pray. Every vocation has its sacrificial nature to it. All vocations are demanding and have their challenges. Jesus desires that we give our all to our call.

While we may all have our own individual and distinct vocation (married life, priesthood, single life), all of us share a common call. This call is really our primary, first, number one call. The call I speak of is to a personal relationship with Jesus. Our true vocation is to know Jesus. Discipleship is everyone's call. As Jesus put it to so many, "Follow me." God calls everyone on the face of the earth to a relationship with him. Then he calls us to live out that relationship in specific ways. We are to be the "salt of the earth" and the "light of the world" in whatever walk of life we find ourselves.

In addition we all share a universal call to holiness. A major part of holiness is to become a loving person. In addition, holiness means to be set apart for God and his use. In order for that to happen, God will be at work sanctifying and purifying us through the people and circumstances of our vocations. You will not be able to run from this. Transformation will occur in whatever walk of life you choose. It is important that each of us becomes holy. This is the meaning of our life's journey.

IT'S FOR YOU!

For many years, I had a prayer talk that I loved. At the beginning of my talk, I would have a cell phone ring. I picked it up and pretended it was from my mother. "Why are you calling me now?" I would say. I politely hung up on her telling her I was busy at the moment. At the very end of my talk, the phone would ring again. When I picked it up I acted as if it were my mother again. "Mom, I told you I was busy. Why are you calling me again?" Suddenly, I realized something and looked afraid. I held the phone at arms length and stared at it in disbelief. After a bit of a hesitation I held it out to all the people in the church and said, "*It's the Lord.* He wants to talk to *you!*"

Don't wait for a phone call to verify that you have a vocation from God! You *are* called. You *have been* chosen. If you are young and still not sure, seek Jesus and you will find and discover what your vocation is. God will never dupe you. He is faithful. Once you find your vocation, live that vocation to the full by following and proclaiming Jesus. "You are a chosen race, a royal priesthood, a holy nation, God's own people, that you may declare the wonderful deeds of God who called you out of darkness into his marvelous light." (1 Pet. 2:9) This book is about experiencing and getting in touch with the light that is God. God is light and in him there is no darkness. (1 Jn.1:5) I have experienced the darkness and now bask in God's marvelous light. Thank you, God, for calling all of us before we were even born.

8
R.S.V.P.

When I was ordained a priest on June 29, 1991, I sent out invitations to the ceremony. Along with the details of the ordination was the request that the person receiving it come to the celebration. In order to be prepared for the meal that followed, we had to know approximately how many would be in attendance. Included with the invitation was another, smaller card and envelope, which asked for a positive or negative response.

I remember when these R.S.V.P. envelopes started coming back to me. I was excited to open them to see who was coming. Many of my friends responded in a positive manner. Their presence at my celebration confirmed and ratified our existing relationship. But I also experienced disappointment when people I thought were close to me responded by saying they couldn't make it. I found myself thinking, "Wait a minute. I thought we were good friends. After all, it's my ordination. I would have thought that so-and-so would come."

In a way we all have been given an envelope with an R.S.V.P. (please reply) from the Lord. He invites us to come to him and to respond to his plan for our lives. He wants us to say "Yes."

After Peter, Isaiah, Moses and Mary encountered God they responded in similar, positive ways. All said "Yes." Isaiah said, "Here I am Lord, send me!" During the ordination rite, the director calls the name of the ordination candidate. The rubrics call for the candidate to answer "present" when his name is called. Remembering the words of Isaiah, when my name was called at the ordination, I responded instead with a loud, "Here I am!"

Peter left his boat, his nets and even his parents and followed Jesus. Luke highlights his thorough response by saying, "They left *everything* and followed Jesus." (Lk. 5:11) The invitation by Jesus was met by an instantaneous, radical, total "Yes" on the part of Peter and his friends.

The Virgin Mary also had her encounter with the divine in the form of the Angel Gabriel. Like the others she became afraid and was invited to surrender by bearing God's son. In words that have become the object of poetry, song and sermons her famous response was, "Behold I am the handmaid of the Lord; let it be done to me according to your word." (Lk. 1:38) Could Mary have possibly known at her "fiat" the suffering that this "Yes" would entail? The horrible prophecy of Simeon cast light on the cost of any "Yes" to God. "A sword will pierce through your own soul also." (Lk. 2:35)

When I led the pilgrimage to the shrines of Italy in 2002, I took 25 people with me. One woman from the mountains of California came primarily to see the *Pieta* in St. Peter's Basilica. The *Pieta*, of course, is the captivatingly beautiful statue of Mary holding the dead Jesus cradled in her lap. It freezes in time the moment when the body of the Son of God was lowered from the Cross and given to his mother. I had seen Michelangelo's statue many times before. As I watched this woman approach it on the pilgrimage, I saw her begin to weep. Suddenly goose bumps came all over me and I began to weep. This thought crossed my mind at that moment, "How right and just it is that this moment not be lost. The sacrifice of Jesus and the suffering of Mary needed to be captured and viewed by millions." Through this statue and through all time, God has honored Mary's "Yes." We are also being shown in this magnificent portrayal by the genius Michelangelo just how expensive any "Yes" to God can be. The *Pieta* shows us that no commitment, whether it is being a parent or a priest, is easy.

I DIE DAILY (1 COR. 15:31)

I have entitled this book *Death: The Final Surrender* because I believe that death will be the last of many surrenders to God. If we continue to say "Yes" to God consistently with our lives, our final "Yes" will be at the moment of our death. Our death will not be happenstance, but a precious return to God. (Ps.116:15) Instead of our life being wrenched from us, we will be yielding it back to God.

Paul the Apostle wrote about "dying daily." Dying, for him, meant exercising self-control and suffering for the Gospel. He was speaking about the crucifixion of the flesh and surrendering his will to God each day. He spoke of his sufferings for Christ as a form of surrender. He wrote about self-sacrifice, determination and discipline. We must understand that surrender is first of all an act of the will. It is a choice that makes us rise above our feelings. As we do it over and over, day after day, it becomes an attitude. Then, when we consistently abandon ourselves to God and his will for our lives, it becomes a lifestyle.

In order to live well, we must be surrendering our wills and our energies to God each day. Mark writes in his Gospel, "If anyone would come after me, let them deny themselves, take up their cross, and follow me." (Mark 8:34) Luke put it well when he nuanced Mark's earlier version by adding one word, "daily." "Take up your cross *daily*." (Lk. 9:23) In other words, Luke is plainly revealing that surrendering yourself to the demands of discipleship is not a one-time or even once a week affair. Christianity is a lifestyle of self-denial and constant surrender. The opportunities for surrender are endless. The call we have is to say "Yes" one day at a time, all the time.

What does surrender mean in practical terms? Surrender happens when you watch less T.V. and spend more time in prayer. It is admitting you are wrong sometimes and saying you are sorry. Abandonment means service, forgiveness and generosity. Yielding to God's will means allowing God to have your thoughts and imaginations. We must also yield our emotions to God. Surrender implies acknowledging God in all your decisions. Morally it means submitting your eyes, ears and mouth to God. It is obedience and submission to the authority in your life. Giving God your time and energies is a great way to surrender. A disciple must be willing to suffer for Jesus. We must be bold enough to risk rejection by speaking about Jesus. Surrender means sacrifice. There are endless areas where we must die to self so that Jesus can be all that we are. In the words of John the Baptist, "He must increase and I must decrease." (Jn. 3:30)

I heard a story about a chicken and pig who were walking down the street together. They saw a starving man sitting by the side of the road begging. At this the chicken turned to the pig and said, "He's famished. Why don't we give him a bacon and egg breakfast?" The pig looked disturbed and replied, "I don't think so. For you that's just an offering, but for me it's a total commitment!"

Christianity is a total 24/7 *commitment*. It is NOT going to church just once a week. It is a daily, hourly, sometimes each moment "Yes" to God.

I was on an airplane and the woman in her 30's next to me struck up a conversation. It didn't take long before I told her I was a priest. Her response was startling. She said, "How long do you do that for – five or ten years?" I smiled and told her, "No, priesthood is a lifelong commitment." I was surprised that she thought that a person becomes a priest for only a few years. Perhaps she thought that if marriage or some other appealing option arose, I could leave the priesthood and then venture out in that direction. I think the idea of a lifelong commitment is foreign to many. Some think that by not having a serious commitment in life they are free. I have found that true freedom comes through your commitment. If you are not committed to something in your life, you are drifting and never really settled within or without. I think that many in our society and culture today are afraid of commitment, fearing the perceived loss of freedom.

I am very encouraged by the multitudes of people who are hungry and thirsty for God. I think this is such an opportune time to be a priest. People want to know about God! Many desire to be committed to Jesus in a deeper way. Scores are going to Bible studies, attending retreats, coming to missions, and reading good spiritual books. Young people everywhere are seeking the truth. They want to reach out to other people and have meaning in their lives. People are tired of being tricked by the world and are seeking the Word instead. Many are getting involved at church and in other ways to help people. People are discovering that Christianity was never meant to be a private thing. Following Jesus means losing your life for others, and thus finding life.

What does surrendering to God daily mean for you? Could it be spending more time in prayer? Is God calling you to read the Bible more? Possibly it means abandoning control of your life to God. Can you step out of the boat and get involved at your local church? Do you believe that God will use you to visit shut-ins or those in the hospital? Is there some idol you need to leave behind so you can go forward?

I hope that through this book, you will sense God's R.S.V.P. invitation to you. He is inviting you to draw near and to surrender to him. He is calling you to salvation and surrender at the Cross. He is calling some to priesthood and the religious life. Others are being called to marriage and the single life. All of us are being called to a deep, intimate relationship with Jesus. As God said so many times throughout the Bible, "Don't be afraid." I invite you to make a new decision to live for Jesus in a quality way. If you "die to self" daily, your real self will live on, even after the day you die. When you surrender to God now, you will find that the hour of your death will simply be the final "Yes" flowing from a lifetime of surrenders. If you continue to resist God, however, your death will be a struggle.

9
DO YOUR BEST, THEN REST

I've always wondered what I would say if I went before God. I am very curious and inquisitive. I am a student of philosophy. I have many questions that beg to be answered. Did Jesus really have to go to the Cross in order to save us or could there have been another way? What about all the suffering in the world? Why didn't God stop the Armenian and Jewish holocausts? What about the deep mysteries of time and eternity? Why was I born at this time and given this specific body? If you came before almighty God what questions would you ask?

Job was a biblical character who found himself in the midst of a lot of personal suffering. If you read the story of Job in the Bible, you will see a man who suffered many things unjustly. Although he had many questions for God, despite his trials he never questioned the existence of God. If you read the book of Job, perhaps you will find yourself asking some of the same questions of God that he asked. I think we have all felt like Job when we see injustice and confusing issues that we cannot understand. Job said, "Oh that I knew where I might find God, that I might come even to his seat! I would lay my case before him and fill my mouth with arguments." (Job 23:3-4)

God finally did answer Job and spoke of his eternal power and magnificence. When Job encountered God's stunning presence, suddenly all his questions melted away and he was left to contemplate God's glory. Job replied, "I know that you can do all things and that no purpose of yours can be thwarted. Therefore, I despise myself, and repent in dust and ashes." (Job 42:2, 6) Suddenly all of Job's deep questions paled when faced with the grandeur and beauty of God. One day "we will know as we are known." (1 Cor. 13:12) All of our pondering, confusion, and deep questioning will find an answer as we contemplate the majesty of God.

When I encountered God in these near death experiences, instead of asking God to solve the mysteries of the universe or to tell me my future, like Job I was more interested in "repenting in dust and ashes." I simply wanted to please God. I realized that although I don't understand all the mysteries of the universe, God does. I don't have to. I love Psalm 131. "I do not occupy myself with things too great and too marvelous for me. But I have calmed and quieted my soul, like a child quieted at its mother's breast; like a child that is quieted is my soul."

After experiencing God's glory, light, voice and love, I knew it was time for me to go back to my body. I had been given a vision of truth. Now I knew God was real. Ever since I was a young boy, I had always had one main question milling about in my mind. The one question I wanted answered more than any other was, "Is there a God or not?" Now I know with *certainty* that God exists and is a rewarder of those who seek him. (Heb. 11:6) God also graced me with direction for my life. From that point on I was to live for God and others and strive to grow in the justification process. I was not given a blueprint for my life anymore than anyone else. My future is a mystery, but it lies in God's hands. I believe he will protect me, as he does all who call upon him, but there is still so much I do not know about my future. Like anyone else, I must live in trust.

As I was about to return to my body it was my turn to speak. I realized that I was going back and God was giving me another chance. I understood that God had allowed me to see his glory and that this vision would be with me forever. Again, I didn't have a "voice," but I was able to convey my thoughts to God. I was aware that as I thought, I was understood by God. I did not ask God a question. I did not ask God for a favor or gift as Solomon did when he had his vision of God. Rather, I made a statement that would color the destiny of my life. I was given the gift to "see the light" and know that God exists. Now I know from whence I came and where I am going. I know that death is not the end but a new beginning. As I was leaving God's presence, I said to God, "Now that I know, I will do the *best!*"

The next thing I knew, I woke up and found myself in my bed. I don't remember the journey back through the tunnel as much as I remember going to God through it. How much time had passed? Not much, because I could hear the sound of the T.V. downstairs. My parents hadn't gone to bed yet. Immediately I began to do something that I can't remember ever doing. I wept. I burst into tears and sobbed. In fact I cried so much that I had to go to the sink and wash my face over and over. Later the thought came to me that when a baby is born it cries. I had been literally reborn and I cried too. The revelation was real, fresh and vivid. I found myself back in my body, alive and well. I was stunned, shocked and trying to grasp what all this meant. My final words to God resounded in my spirit, "Now that I know, I will do my best." My life would never be the same.

It took me years to interpret what these two near death experiences meant. I believe I will spend the rest of my life trying to unpack and live their meaning. For the first ten years of my priesthood, I hardly told anyone of this. I was afraid no one would understand. I was also afraid that if I told others, it would be to bolster myself in their eyes and that God would withhold future revelations from me because of that.

In prayer, I have discerned that it is finally time to speak of what God has done for me and what is to come. I believe God wants his people to know about the death experience. It was given to me for myself and for the people of God. I don't want to go back to that place without having shared the truth of what will happen.

I have often thought about my final statement to God, "Now that I know, I will do my best." What does it mean to do our best for God? I was shopping for a dishwasher in a Sears store some time back. When I got to the appliance department I saw a whole array of different machines. Some were much more expensive than others. Interestingly, there were signs on some of the machines that read "Good" "Better" or "Best." The good dishwashers were less expensive and had fewer features. The best machines had many more features and were the best quality. I believe that we are all called to be our best. What that means for us is that we develop our unique potential and live a quality life filled with the features of energy, excellence and integrity.

MAKING THE MOST OF YOUR LIFE

Being the best means living your life with passion. Strictly speaking passion means suffering, but it can also mean enthusiasm and energy. I think there is nothing more pitiable than someone who is living his or her vocation with a lackluster effort. On the other hand, it inspires me to see priests in their 80's who still have fire. I love it when people who are married and retired get involved in the community and help others. It challenges me when I meet older people who are full of joy and do not regret their past.

In my life I have had to discipline myself and push myself to begin to achieve my potential. That is part of my daily surrender to God. It also gets me out of bed in the morning. One of the areas where I pursue passion is the area of exercise. I take responsibility for my health now and in the future. I try to eat well and exercise often. I run three miles every two or three days. It is especially hard to run into the wind. I remember running on the beach once and the wind was blowing really hard. I kept telling myself, "Don't give up. *Lean* into the wind and press on."

Running and pressing on are apt metaphors for making the most of your life. Paul the Apostle wrote about "running the race and fighting the good fight." (1 Cor. 9:24, 1 Tim. 6:12) Life is a struggle and the wind can be in our face at times. We must keep leaning into it with determination. Paul also put it this way, "Straining forward to what lies ahead, I *press on* toward the goal . . ." (Phil. 4:13-14) Pressing on means standing firm and facing fear when it comes against you. It means learning, doing the work you need to do and being creative. It means setting goals and being determined to see them accomplished. It means being disciplined consistently in all areas of your life. Leaning into it means not giving up when things get hard!

Life is difficult for everyone, not just you. I've learned not to take the things that come against me personally. We are all in this together. God is an equal opportunity employer and the devil is an equal opportunity destroyer. Everyone has to deal with various trials and tribulations. I am not going to let difficulties deter me from achieving and growing and being my best. Obstacles can be opportunities. Day after day after day we are sowing seeds by our attitude and the way we live. Eventually, if we keep it up, we will see results and bear fruit. (Gal. 6:9) The words of Jesus are inspiring, "Be faithful unto death and I will give you the crown of life . . . The one who conquers will sit with me on my throne." (Rev. 2:10, 3:21) We are in a life battle now and the struggle has infinite meaning.

NO PAIN, NO GAIN

As I travel this odyssey called life, I am very aware of major sufferings I go through. I really believe that I have these so that scars can be turned into stars. My sinful self is being put to death and a new creation is emerging. Remember, we are justified and are being justified. God will use the pains, disturbances and thorns in our life to prepare us for our death. As we surrender to God in these "weaknesses," we learn humility and open ourselves up to the working of God.

The scriptural example of this is Paul's "thorn in the flesh." After boasting about his many touches and revelations from God, he humbly brought up the subject of his sufferings.

> And to keep me from being too elated by the abundance of revelations, a thorn was given me in the flesh, a messenger of Satan, to harass me, to keep me from being too elated. Three times I besought the Lord about this, that it should leave me; but he said to me,

"My grace is sufficient for you, for my power is made perfect in weakness." (2 Cor. 12:7-9)

Paul realized that along with the abundance of revelations, his "thorn" was a part of God's plan for his life. It brought him humility in the midst of all his visions. It helped him to rely more on God than on himself. (2 Cor. 1:9) Also, mysteriously, this thorn manifested God's power to mature and sanctify Paul. (Scholars still debate exactly what this thorn was.)

I've also shared with you much of the abundance of my revelations. It makes me feel elated, but I must share the thorn too. In our struggle to become and to be our best, I have discovered that the thorn is God's instrument. God doesn't always remove them but he uses them.

Some say roses have thorns, but I say that thorns have roses. Can you look at the thorn(s) in your life and see God at work through it?

I spoke in my first book *Live Passionately!* about how acne in my teen years deepened me and softened my heart. I became compassionate and less superficial because of this. I know God has turned my flaws into favor and my blemishes into blessings. I still deal with the ravaging effect that acne has had on my psyche and self-image.

In addition, since high school I have suffered with migraine headaches. These particular migraines are the kind that begin with vision impairment. I have even had slurred speech during some headaches. Once the vision impairment moves on, a terrific headache ensues. It can happen anywhere, any time and is totally out of my control.

I have been to the best doctors to try to figure out why this happens and they are at a loss. The best guess is that diet or stress triggers them. It can be awfully scary for me to know that any morning or night, as I am preparing to speak before people, I have the potential to get one of these headaches. If so, I will have trouble seeing the people and may not be able to speak coherently, never mind the pain involved. Although I only get these headaches once or twice a year, this thorn has definitely made me rely on God!

I still suffer occasional panic attacks in front of people. As long as I can remember, I have been nervous and hypersensitive to noise. In addition, I consciously continue to fight against "dreading the future" and "regretting the past." I continue to confront these situations and do not run from them. Running only makes the problems worse. The only way to victory is to go through, not around. (Is. 43:2) I fall on my face before God, in need and dependence. One of the benefits of suffering is that I can teach and preach about these subjects. Because of my sufferings, I have gained a lot of compassion. Compassion is a virtue with an expensive price tag.

God is also using my religious community to draw my best self out of me (although sometimes I think that my worst self is emerging)! Instead of being independent, selfish and self-serving, living in community challenges me to be virtuous. I am under the direction of superiors and am learning the beauty of submission and obedience. I am growing in my concern for the welfare of the brothers I live with. I have to share and give and I can't always have it my way. I am underappreciated at times and struggle to agree with the others on certain topics, yet I find myself praying for my fellow Passionists and concerned about their needs and lives. I know I am being taught humility and I'm growing in a self-esteem that is not determined by people or circumstances. It has much deeper roots than the applause of a crowd.

I've had to surrender to God in all these thorns. Like Paul, I've asked they all be removed. They haven't been taken away. I know that God is faithful so I know there is a reason for everything. God is using these situations to help me die to self, rely on God and live a deeper surrender each day. God detests pride and independence. He wants our trust and surrender. My daily surrender and the positive attitude that I choose in my pain are preparing me for my death. Paul said, "So we do not lose heart. Though our outer nature is wasting away, our inner nature is being renewed every day. For this slight momentary affliction *is preparing for us* an eternal weight of glory beyond all comparison." (2 Cor. 4:16-17)

GO THROUGH, NOT AROUND

Something we all have to understand is that we must "go through." The reason we will have merit when our life is over is because we went through and conquered. In John's heavenly vision, he saw a great multitude from every nation standing before God's throne, clothed in white robes and holding palm branches in their hands. He was told they are those who "*went through* the great tribulation and have washed their robes and made them white in the blood of the Lamb." (Rev. 7:14) In other words, it was the process of going through life on earth that led to their sanctification and victory. The famous Psalm 23:4 tells us, "Even though I walk *through* the valley God is with me." We are not alone in our trials. God is walking with us and using the thorns of life to change us.

Recently I was in a very fearful situation. As I entered it, I heard a whisper in my heart, "I am with you." That made all the difference in the world to me. I was able to go through with God's companionship. The dictionary defines the word "with" as: near to, alongside of, and in the company of. God is near me and I am not alone. Because of God's presence with me I have new courage and strength. I can face my fears, anxieties, hurts and loneliness. I can grow in a healthy self-image even when others don't appreciate me. You can go through successfully also. No matter how hard the circumstance you must endure – divorce, difficult relationships, health problems and even death – you can endure victoriously. Make sure you don't run from hard things or try to go around what God puts in your path. God will be with you as you go through. That's how we gain experience and come to know the ways of God in a deeply personal way.

Don't simply accept life, allow life to challenge you. Look for meaning in everything, especially in your suffering. Choose to have life make you better. Don't abandon the struggle or give up! You will find yourself growing in acceptance and trust and surrender as you go through. These trials are exactly what we need to tease virtue out of us and to diminish the pride which clings so closely.

During my pilgrimage to Italy, one of the favorite stops was the Academia in Florence. The Academia houses some of the greatest artwork in the world, including Michelangelo's *David*. Students still come there to sketch the awesome works done by the master.

While I was there I saw some works that intrigued me and in some ways took my breath away. In that museum we viewed many works that were unfinished. The uncompleted works were statues of people being carved out of a block of granite. The three-quarter finished statues showed the figure of the man or woman still encased in granite. What was so intriguing was how Michelangelo captured the struggle and the wrestling with life. Each of the figures looked as if he or she was straining to emerge from the prison of the granite. In these pieces, I believe Michelangelo was able to put his finger on the pulse of the human condition. All of us struggle and wrestle with life in this world. All of us have some form of thorns. Much like Jacob who wrestled with the angel of the Lord until he was blessed, we can find our trials becoming triumphs if we see the meaning in them and remain positive. Sufferings don't just happen. They are there for a reason and God will use them to bless us if we will let him. As we surrender to God in our struggles, God is preparing us for our final surrender.

HOW DO YOU SPELL MINISTRY? W.O.R.K.

When I told God I would do my best I meant that I would strive to achieve my potential. I fight against laziness and a negative attitude. I resist being ordinary and lackluster. I loathe mediocrity. I'm not going to just sit back and let everyone else accomplish. I want to be a participant, not just a spectator. God is honored by sacrifice, risk, effort, creativity, work and goals. He then blesses our efforts and makes them fruitful according to his plan and will. You will never achieve your destiny if you are not willing to sacrifice.

Being the best, for me, meant committing myself to God and to the community as a priest. More than that, it means tirelessly preaching and serving with enthusiasm, generosity and joy. It means living in a community and accepting others as they are and forgiving their foibles.

In addition, being the best means living a quality life in terms of character. It is has been very clear to me over the last 25 years that there are three main areas of my life that need work. The first area is my prayer life and developing my relationship with God. The second area is my ministry and living in community. Finally, character development and growth in holiness is of utmost importance. If you want to be the best, you must strive for excellence in all these areas too.

In order to make the most of your life, you must grow in maturity. Character development and growth will not just fall on you, you must work at them. When I see areas of my character that are flawed I constantly ask myself, "How long am I going to be like this? Will I be acting the same way at this time next year? Do I want to live my whole life and die with this flaw in me? What do I need to do to change?" I try to draw lines in the sand and challenge myself not to compromise in various areas. Moral integrity and the avoidance of sin are important. Self-control and self-discipline are so crucial in living a quality life. We naturally gravitate toward pleasure and comfort. Growth in holiness, however, will mean suffering as you exercise self-control.

Being the best, preparing yourself well for death and making the most out of your life requires working on your relationship with God, striving to achieve your goals and dreams, and growing in character.

There is a scene from the movie *Amadeus* that has always haunted me. Antonio Salieri was a gifted musician and very skilled in his ability to play the piano. As the movie unfolds, Salieri meets the flamboyant young Amadeus Wolfgang Mozart. Mozart's ability to play the piano was unparalleled. No one had such creative genius and it all seemed to flow out of him without effort or work. Salieri realized that Mozart was the best and he became bitter and insanely envious. He was no longer the top musician and he knew it. The bitterness ate at him.

Toward the end of the movie a scene took place that was very poignant. As the elderly, disillusioned Salieri was being wheeled out in a wheelchair, he looked at the nurses and staff and made the Sign of the Cross as he shouted, "I absolve you of your mediocrity!"

What Salieri needed to learn was that he didn't have to be the best musician in the world. All he was asked to do was to be the best that *he* could be. Instead of being bitter because someone else was better, he should have concentrated on realizing his own potential and achieving that. Often I will compare myself to other preachers who are better or other ministers who seem more giving and compassionate and I will get envious. While their styles or generosity may help me to learn and spur me toward greater excellence, I simply cannot be who they are. The truth dictates that we can never be the best in the world or the worst in the world at whatever we do. Self-compassion calls us to strive to be the best, but to accept ourselves wherever we fall in between those two extremes.

In the parable of the talents, Jesus said that the servants were given "five talents, two and one, each according to *his ability*." (Mt. 25:15) Notice, three different people were all given three different amounts of talents. In the Gospels, often there is a disparity when in comes to the generosity of God. (Mt. 20:1-16) Scripture never advocates competition, but does exalt ambition. It is very freeing to know that I don't have to compare myself with everyone all the time. I have my own unique and specific gifts and talents. I didn't ask to be a preacher, God called me. There will be others who may be more effective, but no one can do it like me. My call is to develop my talents and potential to be the best *I* can be.

When I get to the end of my life I don't want to look back at what could have been. I don't want to say to myself, "I wish I had worked harder or been more creative or risked more." I detest mediocrity. I am working hard to develop my potential. Make no mistake about it: it is work! God has called me, you and everyone else to live passionate, excellent lives. Make the most of your opportunities now. Your efforts will come back to bless you and prepare you for your future. I encourage you to fight the good fight, run the race and press on! If the wind is against you, lean into it. Life is not a dress rehearsal. We only get one chance at this and we must make it count. Be committed to do your *best* for God!

If we become and do our best, we can look forward to rest when we hear the words of Jesus, "*Well done* good and faithful servant. You have been faithful over a little, I will set you over much; enter into the joy of your master." (Mt. 25:21) Hearing those words will be the beginning of the ecstasies of heaven!

10
GRAVE RUBBINGS

I heard a story about a wealthy woman who entered into heaven. St. Peter gave her a bicycle to ride around the streets of gold. As she pedaled around, she saw her butler drive by in a limo and her gardener driving a Jaguar. She was extremely agitated and went to St. Peter complaining about the disparity of travel. St. Peter replied, "The mode of transportation you are assigned in heaven depends on what type of Christian you were on earth." A few days later she came back to St. Peter and she was laughing. "What's so funny?" St. Peter asked. She replied, "I just saw my pastor going by on a pair of roller skates!"

We are not saved by our good works, but by the death and resurrection of Jesus on the Cross for us. However, being saved is more than just praying a prayer of surrender. It is a *lifestyle of surrender* in faith and in deeds, over and over, day by day, that justifies us and puts us right with God. It is our lifelong cooperation with God's grace and abandonment to his will that readies and prepares us for what is to come. We must keep asking ourselves, "Who is the person I want to become?" Having a goal of who we want to be will help us in our day-to-day choices.

A classic story that has touched my life deeply is Charles Dickens' *A Christmas Carol.* The main character in the story is Ebenezer Scrooge. Scrooge was miserly, selfish, uncaring, and had a bad attitude. His classic line, even on Christmas Eve, was "Bah, humbug!" Such was his approach to life. He had an accountant working for him named Bob Cratchit. Scrooge was very cruel toward him.

One Christmas Eve night, the ghost of his dead business partner, Jacob Marley, appeared to him. It was the ghost of a man tormented, in regret and wearing chains. Ebenezer questioned the ghost about his chains. "Tell me why you are fettered?" asked Scrooge. "I wear the chains I forged in life," replied the ghost. "I made it link by link, yard by yard. I girded it on of my own free will and of my own free will I wore it." Such poignant words.

Marley predicted that three more spirits would visit Scrooge. First Scrooge was visited by the ghost of Christmas past. He showed Scrooge his prior upbringing and helped give him insight into why he behaved the way he did. The second ghost was the ghost of Christmas present. Through this ghost Scrooge would learn compassion. He saw the plight of his employee Bob Cratchit and of Bob's son, the crippled Tiny Tim. Previously, he hadn't cared enough to even find out about Cratchit's children. Scrooge was so miserly he didn't even want to give Cratchit Christmas Day off from work!

Lastly came a ghoulish figure. This spirit was a black phantom. He was a draped, hooded, silent figure that resembled the grim reaper. This was the ghost of Christmas future. Whenever Ebenezer asked him a question, all he would do was silently point forward. First they passed by some people in the street talking about someone who just died. They laughed as they gossiped about how cheap he was. That someone who died was Scrooge!

Scrooge and the silent ghost ended up at a dark, shadowy graveyard. The ghost pointed to a tombstone. Ebenezer knew the truth of what he was about to read but didn't want to look. In repentance he cried out, "Men's courses will foreshadow certain ends, to which, if persevered in, they must lead. But if the courses be departed from, the ends will change. Say it is thus with what you show me!" He was pleading for another chance. He begged for more time. The phantom kept pointing at the stone. Then with horror Ebenezer read his own name on the tombstone. He knew that he had died without really living. He knew that his life had been a sorrowful travesty.

Suddenly he awoke and he was in his own bedroom. He realized that he still had more time and he wanted to make good on his promise. It was still Christmas Day! He began laughing like he hadn't in years. "I don't know what day of the month it is!" said Scrooge. "I don't know how long I've been among the spirits. I don't know anything. I'm quite a baby. Never mind. I don't care. I'd rather be a baby. Hallo! Whoop! Hallo here!"

In his glee he began to bless people. He bought the biggest turkey and gave it to Bob Cratchit. When Bob came into work later that Christmas Day he pretended he was angry because Cratchit was late, then laughingly changed his attitude and gave him a raise. He began to truly live as he was capable. He was given more time and he made the most of his life. He began a process of becoming a loving, caring, generous person.

Dickens' story *A Christmas Carol* is moving for me because in many ways it is my story. I believe that now that you have read this book it is *your* story too. My vision of God was meant to change me. It was meant to soften me. It was meant to grace me to treasure the gift of life. I was given such a dramatic vision because so often I can be like Scrooge: selfish, petty, cynical, grumbling and non-caring. I can be my own worst enemy and despise my life. Coming face-to-face with God has broken those chains for me. I'm not yet perfected, but I am pressing on with the goal before me. I still have to make a daily choice to love, treasure and appreciate my life. I can easily revert to the "old" me. Knowing that one day I will again come face-to-face with God helps me change. "Lord, teach us to number our days and gain wisdom of heart." (Ps. 90:12) I feel like a man who has come back from the dead with a message to preach! (Lk. 16:31)

Back in junior high school our English teacher had us do a project. She wanted us to do a grave rubbing. The project involved getting some rice paper and a charcoal crayon. Then I had to select an old tombstone from one of the Massachusetts graveyards. I placed the rice paper over the slab and then rubbed the charcoal crayon lengthwise over it. Instantly all the markings on the headstone appeared on the rice paper. It was like a photographic negative of the tombstone, portable enough to bring to class. We have some pretty old graveyards in western Massachusetts where I grew up. I saw one grave in Old Deerfield that simply had a stone over it with the word "Ma – 1699" etched into it. The one I rubbed was from the early 1800's. I tried to find one that had a lot of information that the years had not faded away.

Most stones have the person's name on them. If the deceased was religious there might be a quote such as "The Lord is my Shepherd." The tombstones of Christians almost all have some type of cross on them. Some people try to announce their philosophy of life or give advice. All, though, have the date of birth and the date of death with a hyphen (-) separating them. That hyphen is perhaps the most important mark on the gravestone. God isn't so much interested in the year you were born and the year you will die, he is interested in what happened in between.

That little dash signifies everything that the person did in his or her life.

What will your dash contain?

You are writing the contents of your dash now.

MORE TO COME

One of the purposes of this book was to look the inevitability of death squarely in the face. I have definitely not denied it or avoided it, but examined it in a way you may never have thought of before. This book has invited you to surrender your life to Jesus and to accept the salvation Jesus offers. I want you to know where you are going and enjoy blessed assurance.

One of my goals is to give you a glimpse into the beyond. I am hoping to relieve you of your fear that death will be the annihilation of your life. I want you to know there is so much more to come. Because we are followers of the one who said "I am the resurrection and I am life," we believe that death is but a new beginning. I have tried to demonstrate, from my own experience, the certainty and glory of life beyond the grave. I pray that the story of my experiences thrilled you and inspired you with glorious hope!

My near-death experiences and this book itself have been about life *here and now* as well as in the hereafter. We have the precious gift of time now, although we don't know for how long. The person we are and the person we become will determine our eternity. Yes, we are saved and justified by our faith in the blood of Jesus who died for us on the Cross. But we are also *being* justified by the way we live our life and how we allow God to take control. Growth in character requires a series of surrenders. It means abandoning ourselves to God each and every day. Death is on the horizon and will be our final surrender. If we live well now we will die well later and experience the final healing.

We are going to die. That is a given. I heard about a man who was mowing his lawn. His foot got a little too close to the blade and it caught his big toe and sliced it off. He got a small box for the toe and had a funeral service for it. Over the grave he put a sign, *More to come later!*

The words of Ebenezer Scrooge when he saw his own tombstone are gripping. "Men's courses will foreshadow certain ends, to which, if persevered in, they must lead. But if the courses be departed from, the ends will change." There is still time for the ends to change as we change. Our finite lives now are of infinite value and have tremendous meaning. What we do now matters. The judgment is now. Our deeds follow us. Our choices and character will determine our eternity. We can literally change our destiny by the way we live today.

Now is the time to seize the day. Don't participate in self-sabotage; love your life! Appreciate the fact that you are gifted and called. Be your own best friend. Live with passion. Keep abandoning yourself to Jesus every day, and allow him to change you one day at a time. Set goals and develop your potential. Be selfless, caring and generous. *Love!* Be the *best you you can be! Then on the day you die, you will be ready for death, the final surrender.*

I am sure that God who began a good work in you will bring it to completion at the day of Jesus Christ. (Phil. 1:6)

THE CONGREGATION OF THE PASSION

The Passionists are a religious community in the Catholic Church. They were founded in 1741 in Italy. The founder of the Passionists was Paul Daneo (St. Paul of the Cross). Their headquarters is in Rome, Italy. They are in 56 countries around the world. The major ministry of the Passionist priests, brothers and sisters is prayer and evangelization.

A Passionist religious professes vows of poverty, chastity, and obedience. Along with these is the unique first vow of a Passionist: to remember and meditate upon the Passion of Jesus and to proclaim its meaning to the world. The sign that Passionists wear on their religious habit (Jesu XPI Passio) means "The Passion of Jesus Christ." A familiar saying of Passionists is: "May the Passion of our Lord be ever in our hearts."

For more information about the Passionists or if you are interested in a religious vocation, please contact:

Vocation Director
Passionist Community
773-631-6336

Websites:
www.passionist.org
www.frcedric.org

WORKS CONSULTED

The New Oxford Annotated Bible with the Apocrypha. Revised Standard Version. ©1973, 1977 by Oxford University Press

Catechism of the Catholic Church ©1994 by Paulist Press

Betty J. Eadie, *Embraced By The Light* (Carson City: Gold Leaf Press, 1992)

Raymond A. Moody, Jr., M.D. *Life After Life* (New York: Bantam Books, 1988)

Raymond A. Moody, Jr., M.D. *The Light Beyond* (New York: Bantam Books, 1988)

It is my intent to give credit for use of copyrighted material contained in this book. If such credit has inadvertently been omitted, please contact me at **frcedric@frcedric.org** so subsequent printings will contain the appropriate acknowledgment.

ABOUT THE AUTHOR

Fr. Cedric Pisegna, C.P. is a Passionist priest who professed vows in September 1985. He was born in Springfield, Massachusetts and graduated from the University of Massachusetts at Amherst with B.S. in Social Work and a minor in Business. In addition, he has studied Philosophy at Southern Illinois University and has studied Speech and Drama at Northwestern University in Chicago. Fr. Cedric graduated from the Catholic Theological Union at Chicago in May 1990, receiving his Master of Divinity degree with Bible Specialization. He was ordained a priest on June 29, 1991.

Presently, Fr. Cedric preaches retreats and missions throughout the United States and Canada, ministering out of the Passionist retreat complex in Houston, Texas. He has preached over 400 missions for 25 years. Fr. Cedric produces a program for TV & Radio, *Live with Passion!*, which presently airs nationally and internationally on the Trinity Broadcasting Network (TBN) and other networks. He has numerous CDs and DVDs on Christian living and has authored eighteen books.

If you would like to share a testimony, help received from this book, or to schedule a mission in your parish, contact Fr. Cedric at:

Fr. Cedric Pisegna, C.P.
430 Bunker Hill Rd.
Houston, TX 77024

E-Mail: frcedric@frcedric.org

INSPIRATIONAL TEACHINGS BY FR. CEDRIC PISEGNA, C.P.

Books:

1   Live Passionately!
2   Glorious Holy Spirit
3   Thy Kingdom Come!
4   You Can Change
5   Death: The Final Surrender
6   Come Encounter Jesus
7   Golf & God
8   Eucharist: A Living Sacrifice
9   God's Not Boring!
10 A Retreat with Fr. Cedric
11 He Touched Me
12 You Can Be Happy: A Lifestyle of Well-Being
13 Kept in Christ
14 Seasons of Life
15 The Sacred Walk
16 Choose Life and Live!
17 Rise! Living the Risen Life
18 You Are Loved!

Additional Inspirational Teaching Series:

Fr. Cedric has produced hundreds of CDs and DVDs that will deepen your relationship with God and inspire you to Live with Passion!

To place an order online or for a complete listing of Fr. Cedric's teachings visit
www.frcedric.org

For ordering by mail contact:
JC Productions • Jim & Janice Carleton
2931 N. Willamette Blvd.
Portland, OR 97217 • 844 FatherC - (844-328-4972)
E-mail:Jim@frcedric.org • Website:www.frcedric.org

✝ Notes ✝

✝ Notes ✝

✝ Notes ✝